It Co

Terry Manners, forty-eight, is Assistant Editor of the *Daily Express*. For six years he was Night Editor of the newspaper, controlling the coverage of all the major stories from the Lockerbie disaster to the Gulf War.

He wrote the first book on the Gulf conflict which sold out in the first month of publication. His book on the life story of millionaire gambler Alex Bird reached number six in the *Daily Mail* list of hard-back bestsellers.

Before joining the *Daily Express*, Terry was on the editorial staff of *The Guardian*.

He is a Barker of the Variety Club of Great Britain and has been a member of the Press Association's panel of consultant editors for a number of years. He lives with his wife and family on the Essex coast.

His book *Deadlier Than The Male: Female Serial Killers* was published by Pan in October 1995, while *Rhys: The Fight for Life* has recently been published by Virgin Books.

It Could Be You!

*Remarkable True Stories
of the
Lottery Jackpot Winners*

Terry Manners

HEADLINE

First published in 1995
by HEADLINE BOOK PUBLISHING

First published in paperback in 1995
by HEADLINE BOOK PUBLISHING

10 9 8 7 6 5 4 3 2 1

ISBN 0 7472 5250 5

Typeset by
Letterpart Limited, Reigate, Surrey

Printed and bound in Great Britain by
Cox & Wyman Ltd, Reading, Berks

HEADLINE BOOK PUBLISHING
A division of Hodder Headline PLC
338 Euston Road
London NW1 3BH

To my wife Carol for the long nights of typing and to Jackie Holland for all her painstaking research.

Also to all the commuters on British Rail's 'Misery Line' between Shoeburyness and Fenchurch Street. May you all win the National Lottery jackpot so that you don't have to suffer any more.

Finally thank you to the National Press particularly the *Daily Express*, the *News of the World* and the *Sun*. As always they have been a fund of ceaseless information. Without the freedom of the media our little bit of the world would be a very austere place.

Contents

Foreword

It could be you – but it probably won't be. Most people dream of winning the multi-million pound National Lottery jackpot and telling the boss just what to do with his job. As the clock ticks on towards the big draw on a Saturday night, millions of us fantasise about buying a Rolls-Royce car, cruising in the Caribbean, toasting our success with champagne or simply paying off the mortgage. But by the time the last pink ball rolls down the chute of the draw machine Merlin, all we are left with is the smile on bubbly TV presenter Anthea Turner's face and our dreams have turned as grey as Noel Edmonds' beard. The odds on hitting the jackpot are around fourteen million to one, but talking about how to spend our winnings has replaced the weather in idle British chatter. Before the lottery there were fifteen million regular gamblers in the United Kingdom. Now there are twenty-five million. But what happens from the moment your numbers come up on the TV screen?

What next? Are all your worries over or just beginning? Here, with the help of some lottery insiders, we go behind the scenes as the big winners pop their champagne.

Chapter One

Lottery Potty

The man from Camelot pushed his multi-million pound lottery winner over the back-garden fence, apologising for standing on the evergreen shrubs. Mukhtar Mohidin, nicknamed Mr Vindaloot by the Press before they knew his real identity, wasn't listening. He could hardly speak from the shock of winning £17.8 million. He had trusted his friends to keep his good fortune quiet. And they had for two days. But now a battery of photographers and reporters stood at the front door of the £50,000 semi-detached house he had worked so hard to buy. The hacks were pleased with themselves; it had been a hard and exciting hunt and they had found their prey.

The white knight from Camelot was a former Fleet Street hack himself. He just couldn't believe his former counterparts had not covered the rear of the house. Thirty minutes later they were there in force . . . but it was too late. Camelot Man, clutching his mobile telephone, had spirited the biggest prize-winner in the history of Britain away to his mother's home. But the drama didn't end there.

Camelot Man had to return to pick up Mukhtar's suitcase and what he saw made him smile. But that is another story in the long catalogue of the nation's big draw winners. When the white knight pushed Mukhtar Mohidin over the fence, he pushed him into another world . . . the world of the lottery-age millionaires.

The blazing comet left a sparkling trail as it shot across space towards Planet Earth and night-time Britain. As it sped through the darkness it suddenly burst into a vast, shining, translucent golden hand. The hand spurned fishermen on their trawler, a lonely canal boat on a high aqueduct, a little girl at her bedroom window, and an unwitting passenger on British Rail. Finally it tapped a huge finger on a London flat window and a sepulchral voice announced to the stunned occupant, 'It's You!'

The enormous digits then turned into a firework display across the London sky with the legendary Camelot phrase, 'It Could Be You.'

It was the biggest advertising campaign ever to sweep the United Kingdom. Over fifteen days, more than forty million adults saw Saatchi and Saatchi's TV commercial an average of thirteen times each. The advertisement, which took seven weeks of round-the-clock work to make, was centred on real locations – South Stack Lighthouse and Heather Hill in Anglesey, the Llangollen aqueduct and a number of locations around Edinburgh. The theme was developed after national research showed that what best symbolised the National Lottery in people's minds was crossed fingers.

Lottery madness had begun and it was here to stay.

The build-up to the National Lottery started on 4 November 1994 with more Saatchi and Saatchi advertising.

'The symbol of the crossed fingers sums up the anticipation and the feeling that someone has to win,' said Camelot's Commercial Director Norman Hawkins. The symbol was named 'The Hand of Good Fortune'.

Meanwhile the slogan 'It Could Be You' also appeared on 3,000 poster sites, totalling 660,000 square feet throughout the United Kingdom. An estimated thirty-four million adults saw them, nineteen million people heard radio jingles and thirty-nine million read advertisements in the Press.

Camelot refused to reveal even approximate figures of how much it all cost. When pressed, however, they admitted it was the largest single advertising marketing spend ever in the history of the United Kingdom.

'Nobody has launched anything quite like this before,' said Camelot's David Rigg.

Fireworks crackled and the multi-coloured sparks of rockets fell like confetti in the early morning sky over the River Thames as John Major stood smiling in the shadow of the Tower of London.

It was Monday 14 November, and National Lottery tickets were going on sale at last. VIPs, including the Prime Minister and TV presenter Anneka Rice, arrived at the Tower at 6.30a.m. In the eerie half light, with a gale blowing around the deserted battlements, the setting seemed more appropriate to a Shakespearean tragedy than to an event John Major promised would revolutionise life in Britain. For days the National Heritage Secretary, Stephen Dorrell, had been wearing the hassled look of a politician under pressure. His department had overall responsibility for ensuring that the lottery ran smoothly. Or, as he put it, 'We are the assurance that proper standards will be applied – we are the enforcement mechanism.'

In the half light and a chilly November wind, John Major pledged, 'The lottery will unlock the door to a higher quality of life for millions of people, irrespective of income and without extra taxation.'

Up to 250,000 people could win each week – mostly small sums, though there would be a £1 million winner from each draw. Little did he and Camelot realise what the actual numbers and sums would be.

Mr Major reiterated Camelot's hope that over the next seven years the lottery would raise £9 billion for the arts, sports, charities, the Millennium Fund and Britain's heritage. The guesstimate was almost four times greater than anticipated in 1992 when the lottery was first being set up.

As cynical onlookers berated the hype and scoffed at the grandiose claims, Ms Rice, the mistress of ceremonies, forgot the name of Sir Ron Dearing, Camelot's chairman, but he pressed on, pressing the plunger to put the lottery computers on-line.

For Sir Ron it was a magic moment. Twice, as head of the Post Office in the 1980s he had proposed a lottery to the then Prime Minister, Mrs Margaret Thatcher, and twice she had turned down the idea. Sir

Ron, who lost his father in the war when he was ten and could not forget his impoverished background as an evacuee in a Yorkshire mining community, had never given up the idea.

He came from a persevering past. The family he lived with would buy stale cakes every Tuesday, three days after they had been baked – because they were cheaper. Now those who scoffed at his dream would soon be eating their losing lottery tickets. For the game was quickly to become a regular fixture of life in Britain. It would even replace the weather as the conversation topic in the office and the shop queue. BBC1 Controller Alan Yentob's vision was coming true. He had characterised the lottery as a shared national experience, like the Grand National or the Last Night of the Proms.

Viewers held their breath and crossed their fingers. The tension was building.

'Tonight we are making television history,' said Noel Edmonds and the studio audience cheered. It was a windswept Saturday evening on 19 November, 1994, and the moment lottery-potty Britain had been waiting for had arrived – the big draw.

The *National Lottery Live* cameras panned in on effervescent co-presenter Anthea Turner, waving from a crowded Tesco supermarket in Nottingham which had sold 12,500 tickets. All over Britain £18,000 a minute was being spent in a last-chance frenzy and stores had drafted in extra staff to keep pace with the surge as the clock marched towards 8p.m. The voices of some churchmen and other critics of the nationwide draw were drowned by the ringing of the cash tills as 15,000 retailers with ticket terminals across the country witnessed the birth of a phenomenon and pocketed five pence in the pound from every punter's dream stake.

At the John Menzies outlet in Weymouth, Dorset, staff were handing out free sweets to placate waiting punters, and as workers at the Texaco Garage in Hungerford, Berks, battled to register tickets, dozens of drivers left without paying for their petrol.

At the BBC Television Centre in London, a Securicor truck arrived with £3 million in banknotes.

'This is what £3 million looks like,' shouted Noel, and again the audience cheered. As he spoke, one man who claimed the lottery was immoral was holding a public meeting to boycott sales in Taunton, Somerset. But only two people turned up – reporters with lottery tickets in their pockets.

At 7.58p.m. student Debbie Walsh from Northwich, Cheshire, who was celebrating her eighteenth birthday, started lottery machine Merlin rolling, and pink and red and blue numbered balls spun in the air. She had been given the honour after winning a studio contest.

'Fifteen, fourteen, thirteen . . .' Noel shouted and the 360-strong studio audience, clutching their lottery cards, among them BBC1 Controller Alan Yentob, counted down the seconds with him.

Pubs across the land went silent as drinkers clustered around TV sets to watch the fifteen-minute show and parents rushed into their living rooms clutching their tickets and lucky charms, praying they would be among the winners who would share the £22 million prize money. More than twenty-five million people had bought £45 million worth of tickets.

The first ball out was number 30. Then came 3, 5, 44, 14 and 22. Plus bonus number 10. The audience went silent for a moment. Not a winner in the house, or so it seemed. But one man was keeping quiet, studio presenter Gordon Kennedy. We would later find out why.

Off camera seven people in Britain were to share a staggering £5.6 million jackpot – a cool £800,000 each. Another thirty-nine won £40,000 apiece and there were 1,100,000 winners in all – around five times more than expected. They picked up a minimum of £10 each. Many of them much more. Strangely, over £600,000 in prize money was never to be claimed by people who had bought winning tickets.

Presenter Noel was also on a winner. He captured one of Britain's largest-ever television audiences of nineteen million viewers for BBC1.

Now presenter Gordon Kennedy's story could be told. Words didn't often fail the TV star, but during that pioneering programme they nearly did.

'The first three numbers that came up were the first three numbers on my ticket,' he admitted. 'I didn't say anything on TV, but I was so fazed by it I went into partial shock in case I was winning the jackpot.' Seconds later Gordon had won just £10.

Among the losers in that first, history-making week, was the Archbishop of Canterbury, George Carey, who risked a pound. A Church of England spokesman said, 'I suppose he did it because it was for a good cause. We have no idea what he would have spent the money on if he had won. But he wouldn't have kept it all for himself.'

The Press were hungry for details and the stories began to roll in. One lottery fanatic had gambled £800 on tickets. The mystery man walked into Woolworths in Newcastle-upon-Tyne and pulled out a roll of cash.

'We thought it was a joke at first,' said a shop spokesman. 'We had never dealt with 800 entries from one person.' He didn't win a bean.

Another store also made history – by becoming the first victim of a National Lottery hold-up. A youth snatched £200 in ticket takings from a woman assistant at Prime Time News in Devonport. And lottery-mania left one shop worker nursing sore legs after an irate, would-be punter whacked her with his walking stick. The elderly man saw red at Regal Enterprises in Minehead, Somerset, because the ticket machine wasn't working.

The path to the first big draw had been as rocky as Saatchi and Saatchi's night-sky comet. Camelot Group plc was the company chosen to take on the huge project, winning the contract in May 1994 against eight other bidders, including a consortium headed by Virgin boss Richard Branson.

Camelot was made up of five companies, each with its own expertise in the operation needed to run the nation-wide game. From advising and protecting the winners to installing ticket machines and hunting the fraud-sters, everything seemed to be covered. Originally Camelot set about creating a network of around 10,000 outlets with computer terminals – mainly in newsagents', post offices, petrol stations and supermarkets – where the £1 lottery tickets could be bought and smaller prizes collected. First and foremost it was important to choose advisers who could reassure the big winners. For this Camelot turned to Fleet Street and called on journalists like Alastair Buchan, formerly of the Daily Star, who became one of the company's leading consultants.

The consortium comprised Cadbury Schweppes plc; De La Rue plc, the world's largest high-security printing company; GTECH UK Ltd, a subsidiary of the world's leading supplier and operator of government lotteries; Racal Electronics plc; and ICL, the leading professional electronics communications company.

Many critics had carped at the government's decision to put the lottery out to tender. But OFLOT, the regulator, argued that Camelot's operational costs and profit take were the lowest of the applicants, including Richard Branson's much-vaunted bid. So the tender invitations had worked after all. It was also stressed that Camelot's £125 million outlay was unlikely to be recouped much before the third year of the licence. The debate raged on.

Then came more bickering. Two months before draw machine Merlin was to make its debut, one of the key elements – the TV show on which major winners would be announced each week – had still not been agreed. Senior executives at the BBC, which won the contract for the programme after ITV was ruled out from applying, were frustrated that they had not been able to reach agreement with Camelot and OFLOT.

BBC1 Controller Alan Yentob and Head of Entertainment David Liddiment were expecting their Saturday night programme to draw more than twenty million viewers, making it the most popular show of the week. This would help boost BBC1's overall audience, currently lagging behind ITV. But by September there were still no decisions over the format of the show and the Corporation had not been able to make any pilots.

Things heated up. There were round-the-clock discussions over whether the show would be a new, purpose-made lottery programme running for about thirty minutes, or integrated within an existing successful format, such as Noel Edmond's *House Party* or Bruce Forsyth's *Generation Game*. There were also talks about a possible midweek show.

Another problem was that the winning numbers became public property when they were announced on the air. That meant that ITV, Channel Four and Sky could immediately superimpose the numbers on screen during their own programmes. Viewers could still watch, say, Cilla Black's *Blind Date* on ITV, and check if they had won the jackpot. TV bosses had also drawn a blank in their bid to attract a big-name host for the weekly, live National Lottery draw. Some stars were unwilling to be involved.

Time was running out. With two months to go before Britain's first multi-million pound jackpot winner was unveiled, the format of the show had yet to be decided.

BBC bosses – believed to have bid £3 million for the rights to screen the draw – gave producer Michael Leggo the unenviable task of coming up with ideas. He was the man behind the hugely successful TV series *Noel's House Party* and the creator of Mr Blobby, the full-size, pink balloon character who was an almost nationwide family favourite. But even his plans were frustrated in finding the right person to host the programme.

The favourite, Noel Edmonds, had already ruled himself out of the running. *Big Breakfast* star Chris

Evans and *Generation Game* host Bruce Forsyth were understood to have refused similar offers. *House Party* star Edmonds was reportedly worried that he would be over-exposed if he agreed to host the fifty-one-week-a-year show. He was said to have been approached by his close friend Leggo and offered a lucrative deal – but turned it down. Multi-millionaire Edmonds told Leggo he believed the job was too big for one presenter and that he didn't need the money. He was also busy working on his own Saturday night show and other new TV projects.

BBC bosses drew more blanks with other stars on the short list . . . chat-show anchormen Michael Aspel, Terry Wogan and the ever-active Chris Tarrant. *Take Your Pick* host Des O'Connor had been lined up if ITV won the bid, with Michael Barrymore and GMTV's Eamonn Holmes also in the frame.

Bruce Forsyth's manager said the *Generation Game* star's new exclusive deal with ITV ruled him out of the job. But he admitted, 'It is unlikely Bruce would have been interested. It has the potential to be a poisoned chalice. Anyone hosting the show is in danger of becoming typecast.'

The BBC was pressed by the Press and a spokesman admitted, 'We are still holding talks with Camelot about the programme. Unfortunately we are not in a position to announce exactly what the format of the Saturday night show will be. It is still too early for us to say anything or give any indication about who will present the slot.' The clock marched on.

Then out of the *Blue Peter* blue, a Camelot spokesman ruled out the likelihood of a big-name star presenting the programme. He said, 'We want someone fresh and new.' The mystery deepened.

Finally, at the eleventh hour, all was revealed. On 18 October, it was announced that the blonde GMTV presenter Anthea Turner and comic actor Gordon Kennedy had jointly landed the job. Noel Edmonds would launch the first show on 19 November, but then thirty-six-year-old Gordon and former *Blue Peter* hostess Anthea would take over, handling the live draws at venues around Britain.

Edinburgh-born Gordon had only worked on late-night TV shows until then. He was last seen on television in the Channel Four comedy *Absolutely* and presenting Carlton TV's *Big City* magazine show. He was amazed when he was picked.

'It's very exciting and a bit daunting doing something of this size,' he said. 'But Anthea has a firm hand on the tiller so it will be fun. It was strange how it happened. One day the BBC called me into a meeting and told me all about the National Lottery. I was really interested because I did not know much about it. I was expecting to make a documentary on the subject, but they asked me to co-host the programme.'

Gordon had suddenly come a long way from his £350-a-show job with Russ Abbot in 1986.

Fellow lottery host Anthea, was also thrilled about the new role. She said, 'It's a great honour. I only heard at the weekend. It will the latest craze to hit the nation and will be a guaranteed success.' She intended to combine the show with her job as GMTV presenter. 'I'll still be getting up at four o'clock in the morning,' she said, smiling as ever.

But the strain would soon begin to show for the bubbly presenter whose favourite drink was Ribena and who counted among her friends a childhood teddy bear.

After weeks of bad publicity, complaints about shortages of terminals, worries that the jackpot was too large and that charities, betting shops, Pools firms and bingo halls would lose out, Camelot faced another nightmare scenario at the hands of the critics.

As the queues snaked their way around Asda and the Co-op to buy tickets, some church dignitaries and politicians claimed the poor were being encouraged to waste their money to subsidise the pastimes of the rich. But gradually they were consoled by the thought that some of the money gambled would go to good causes. For every pound spent on National Lottery tickets, twenty-eight pence was to be divided between the arts, charities, sports, national heritage and the Millennium Fund.

Many people who supported the launch of the lottery believed that more was going to charities, which expected to lose money because people were buying tickets rather than making donations to the needy. In Ireland, for example, the launch of the State Lottery led to a four per cent drop in giving to worthy causes.

Camelot denied that charities would be affected and said that people would differentiate between giving and paying for lottery tickets. But any hopes that charities would be among those who would benefit quickly from the money raised from the game were dashed by the slowness in setting up the National Charities Lottery Board.

While the Sports Council, the Arts Council and the National Heritage Fund had application forms ready and were set to start handing out cash by March 1995, charities would not see any money for at least a year.

The Lottery Board had a chairman – Marks and Spencer director David Sieff – but it had no chief executive, had yet to open a bank account or work out how it would deal with around 200,000 applications a year. Mr Sieff stressed it was important that the right organisation was in place before a decision was made on who would get any money.

'Whether we are going to benefit the community in three months' time or nine months' time makes no difference,' he said.

Soon the concerns of the churchmen and those in the voluntary sector were silenced by the weight of public opinion. If sales continued at the initial phenomenal rate, it appeared that the good causes would each benefit by £1.6 million.

John Major told the nation that he hoped every person would gain in some way, whether it was a school looking for a soccer pitch or a village hall with a leaking roof.

And, of course, the retailers would gain too. Ticket terminals across the nation were sizzling and the margin on sales of five per cent was being achieved with minimum effort. According to the marketing men, it was 'almost pure profit, going straight to the bottom line'.

Before the lottery launch, Saturday was the busiest day of the week for most retailers, accounting for twenty-five per cent of the week's sales. Now the lottery was to gear trading even more towards the weekend, with two-thirds of trade squeezed into Friday and Saturday, when seventy per cent of the tickets were sold. With an additional twelve million trips to the shops being made each week, lottery stores began to see sales rise by between six and twenty per cent. And there was an increase in impulse purchases too, such as crisps, chocolate bars and magazines, snapped up as treats by people as they queued.

But supermarkets became the main beneficiaries of the boom, attracting thirty-three per cent of purchases, with local grocers' shops and confectioners' attracting fourteen and fifteen per cent respectively.

Her jewellery was by Cartier and her hair by Nicky Clarke but her jumpers were by Naf Naf and she drove a Golf GTI convertible. Enter Miss Camelot, Anthea Turner. But by the end of 1994 the mildly dyslexic young lady from Stoke-on-Trent with seven O-levels, two A-levels, the shiniest TV teeth in Britain and the sexiest legs, wasn't smiling much behind the scenes any more.

Children thought of her as a big sister, even though she was thirty-five. Middle-aged men sighed at her girliness. Women found her straightforward, honest and decent. But the critics weren't impressed.

While things were going from strength to strength for Camelot, the story was turning sour for the BBC again. By 21 December a shake-up had been ordered for the Corporation's 'amateurish' *National Lottery Live* programme. Boss Alan Yentob said he wanted to inject excitement into the show, which he admitted was disappointing. He set out a list of improvements to win back BBC1 viewers after ratings dropped from 19 million to 17.6 million. Presenters Anthea and Gordon came under attack for fluffing their lines and not knowing the jackpot total.

In just a few months Anthea had gone from being everyone's favourite kid sister to being the nation's Aunt Sally. When she left *Blue Peter* for GMTV, one critic said it was 'a rare example of a presenter leaving a children's show and going intellectually down-market'. Now the *Daily Mail*'s Lynda Lee-Potter was calling Anthea 'crashingly dull . . . a bulging-eyed, grinning pixie in a semi-waking nightmare'. Anthea was taking the blame and the stress was beginning to tell.

She tearfully replied, 'I'm not given to crying, but it did bring on the tears. I was prepared for a certain amount of criticism, but not the sheer ferocity of it. My first reaction was hurt, followed by anger. Then you have to put it into perspective and ride with it. You look at the viewing figures and say, "Well, who's right? Do we make programmes for the critics or the public? If the show is so bad, why don't people just watch the numbers come up on Cilla Black's *Blind Date* on the other side?" I don't have to prove anything to some people. But I have something to prove to myself and to the people who have put their faith in me.'

What hurt Anthea most was when *Today* news-paper's Anne Robinson said she hoped the lottery would not involve her reading out any words 'because she knows very few'.

Anthea's bright eyes clouded over as she said, 'I found that particularly offensive because I am dys-lexic. I was very angry. It wasn't just another slight

I could ignore. And I know from the reaction I got from viewers that it upset a great many people who are dyslexic too, or who have dyslexic children. When I am called thick or empty-headed, it is exactly what a lot of unfortunate children have had to go through in school.'

Anthea's dyslexia was diagnosed when she was thirteen, at her comprehensive school in her home town of Stoke-on-Trent, Staffordshire, where she was dropped down into the slow stream.

'I went from being a happy, outgoing kid to being quiet and withdrawn,' she said. 'In many ways I was fortunate. My reading was always good. It was writing which was a problem, and still is. At middle school, which I loved, I could get away with it. I made up for my disability in other ways, by being good at music and drama.'

Until the autumn of 1994, when Anthea did a series of programmes on GMTV for National Dyslexia Week with Dr Hilary Jones, she had never admitted her disability. Now the criticism of the National Lottery show had stopped her in her tracks.

'I had quite a smooth ride before,' she said. 'No one bothered to have a pop at me for doing *Blue Peter*. That could be because most of the critics are probably doing something else in the afternoon when it's on . . . like still having lunch.'

Soon Gordon and Anthea announced they would be leaving the programme when their six-month contracts expired.

'Like most people, I'm riddled with self-doubt,' admitted Anthea. 'And some of the things that have been written have really got to me. But I did not quit.

I'm leaving in March because I only ever signed on for seventeen programmes. It would be physically impossible to stay longer.

'GMTV is my day job, five days a week, and it's very demanding. I'm up at four o'clock every morning. The lottery takes up my weekends, which are my only opportunity to get some sort of normal life.'

Anthea told how her four-year marriage to former DJ turned showbusiness manager Peter Powell, was rock solid but said, 'He often finds himself working nights – when I'm already tucked up in bed. Before Christmas, I didn't see Peter at all for ten days.'

She saw the end of her lottery stint as 'the light at the end of the tunnel'. Privately she had reservations about the National Lottery show, but was far too polite to express them in public, apart from saying, 'It has to be a changing show, one which will re-invent itself and re-emerge every so often in a different form.'

When she and Gordon left, who should take over?

'Oh, Anne Robinson and Lynda Lee-Potter of course,' said Anthea smiling through the hurt. 'Let's see what they can do with it.'

There were some high-ranking journalists on Anthea's side though. One was the venerable Sir John Junor, columnist of *The Mail on Sunday*. He saw Anthea as the National Lottery draw's 'saving grace'. She was not only highly attractive to look at, but had 'quite the best figure and legs on TV'. She fizzed with vitality and gave the impression she actually enjoyed what she was doing, he said, accusing Anthea's female detractors of being motivated by envy. He was later proved to be right. For whenever the lottery made headline news, a picture of Anthea accompanied the story; whenever someone shouted that not enough money was going to charity or that the £1 million a week being creamed off by Camelot smacked of fat cattery, newspapers wheeled out a picture of Anthea and her legs.

The Anthea debate raged on. Yentob had his own views, 'It is a tricky job for anyone to do. We have been experiencing teething problems but we are determined to get it right. We are learning as we go and the show definitely needs some fine tuning. There needs to be less banter and more excitement. We need more winners on the screen, which is what people are interested in.'

Producers had come to realise that the programme posed special problems for television. Viewers couldn't see the jackpot winner at the end of the show, so it was a slot without a punch-line – a big let-down. The main event – the ecstatic winner discovering the moment of truth – took place in a living room well away from the camera lens. Viewers could not share the excitement.

The champagne corks popped and the room at the BBC's Television Centre was filled with laughter. It was 16 February and Anthea was celebrating after agreeing to stay with the TV show. The pressure on her had been great. BBC bosses and Camelot had leant on her to stick with it. Her reward – a doubling of her salary. The bubbly presenter finally signed a deal to host the live Saturday night draw for another six months. She had hit the jackpot, scooping £4,000 for each fifteen-minute show. That was £266 a minute.

The BBC was revamping the much-criticised programme to stop viewers switching over to the other side. Now, instead of travelling around the country, the show was to become permanently based in a studio in London.

'How can I win the lottery, Anthea?' asked *Darling Buds of May* star, Catharine Zeta Jones, as the cameras rolled.

Anthea smiled and leant over to the actress.

'Just wait until afterwards and I'll tell you, because it's all fixed,' she joked. 'You know they pick the numbers before the show in case the machine breaks down – so I've got them in my pocket.'

Quickly realising the joke had gone too far on her breakfast show, red-faced Anthea added, 'I always think if I say something so bizarre, no one is going to believe me. I think we'd better take a break now.'

The punters were angry. Within minutes they bombarded Camelot with telephone calls. Camelot chiefs insisted Anthea apologise on GMTV.

'We've been tearing our hair out with all the people ringing in,' a spokesman said. 'Joe Public is so into the lottery that any hint it can be rigged gets him worried. We know Anthea was only joking, but it affects our integrity and credibility. The simplest thing is for her to retract what she said.'

Anthea conceded. 'I'm sorry if anyone took me seriously – it's impossible to fix the lottery,' she told viewers. 'People ask me to help them win and I always make the same joke.'

Meanwhile, although Anthea had signed to continue fronting *National Lottery Live*, co-presenter

Gordon Kennedy insisted that he was quitting because he was bored. The Scottish comedian denied the BBC was dropping him. 'I have a short attention span,' he said. 'I'm much better when I keep moving and do different things. Six months is enough.' Kennedy was eager to return to his late-night comedy show, *Absolutely*, and was planning a new sitcom. 'It's magic to get back to acting and comedy,' he said. 'I love it and I missed it when I wasn't doing it.'

The former PE teacher refuted criticism of his performance, insisting he had not made mistakes. 'I never fluffed my lines ever,' he said. 'It's no big deal if someone makes a mistake, but I didn't.'

As another problem was solved, a new one emerged. Research indicated that eighty per cent of lottery purchases were pre-planned. Customers in fifty per cent of cases made special trips to buy tickets and in thirty per cent, buying a ticket was the sole reason for visiting a shop. Some storekeepers weren't happy and a handful of them began to pull out of the lottery, concerned about disruption being caused by large crowds on Friday and Saturday.

One of them was High Street giant Superdrug, which switched off its lottery machines in some outlets after complaints from other customers. The chemist chain said stores had been so full of people wanting to buy tickets that other shoppers were put off buying goods. Superdrug pulled the plug on terminals at three branches – Southend, Islington and South Shields – and was reviewing plans for others.

'These were busy stores and lottery machines brought in a lot of extra customers just for the tickets.

Some genuine customers were agitated because they had to join large queues of gamblers as they tried to buy shampoos and shaving creams. It was very upsetting for them,' a spokesman said.

Superdrug would continue to sell tickets in eight other shops – but put on hold a decision to install terminals in another 600 branches.

As lottery mania grew over the first six months, one syndicate hit the jackpot without buying a ticket.

Camelot revealed that its Chief Executive, Tim Holley, would earn over £1 million in pay and bonuses in just three years. Other top directors would pick up more than £800,000. The consortium had made profits of £10.8 million, slightly lower than predicted, in the financial year to April. Sales for the weekly draw had been £1.19 billion since the launch of 14 November, of which £317 million had been raised for good causes – £90 million more than predicted.

Officials pointed out that had the lottery not been launched on time, the organisation would have faced £1 million-a-day penalty payments.

There was another big kitty too. By the first week in May, lottery prizes totalling £17 million were still unclaimed. Punters only had until 17 May to launch their claim for the first week's winning tickets.

The roll-over jackpots had hit the £18 million mark and the stories of joy and despair began to roll in. Winners went into hiding, their long-lost relatives came out of the woodwork and legal battles over the winning tickets abounded.

Whatever people thought didn't distract from their passion for the lottery. Before it was born on 14 November 1994, there were fifteen million regular gamblers in the United Kingdom. Now there were twenty-five million.

There was only one guaranteed winner at the end of the day – the Treasury.

Chapter Two

It's You!

Out of the Blue – It's You! That's the title of a
secret little document given to just a few members of a very select circle . . . the Camelot National
Lottery Jackpot Club.

The twenty-four-page, full-colour booklet, nicknamed 'The Bible' takes the lucky big-win punter
through the pitfalls of his new world. 'You're probably
still wondering when your feet are going to touch the
ground again!' it says. 'But first things first.'

Everyone may dream of winning the lottery, but
what really happens when the numbers you have
chosen from the bar code on your breakfast packet of
cornflakes flash up on the TV screen? I mean, what do
you do, apart from scream?

First: ring Camelot's National Lottery Line in
Aintree. The telephone number is on the back of your
ticket. They will be waiting for your call on Saturday
evening or Sunday. But don't imagine that there is an

army of Camelot men sitting by the telephone. You will just get voicemail. Press this and that, hash numbers and so on. Finally you should hear something like, 'If you think you have won the jackpot . . . stay on the line.'

The minutes may seem like hours as you desperately hang on to the handset, wondering why your fingers are visibly shaking. Finally, you find yourself talking to a Camelot supervisor. Now you are in the major league. He or she will ask you for details of the ticket, the bar code and so on.

'It's funny,' said a lottery mole, 'winners may be confused, frightened and crouching down on all fours because they believe Fleet Street photographers are already outside their house and have special lenses that can film them through their net curtains, but they always manage to read out the bar code. If there is one thing Joe Public understands it is bar codes.'

Camelot will also want to know where you bought the ticket. A security check will be made to make sure you call is not a hoax. As they begin checking your number on their computer, you are reassured. The Camelot team are following a well-written, and well-rehearsed script.

During the first few weeks of the lottery, Camelot was bombarded with hundreds of call from punters claiming that they had won. Some were hoaxes, you always get them, don't you, others were people who had done more than one line of numbers and believed that even if they got one number per line, as long as they had all six on the ticket, they had won the jackpot.

Camelot will already know which newsagent sold

the ticket to you; every retailer's terminal registers them to a central computer. A little-known fact is that there are three computers, operating simultaneously but independently . . . the mother, a back-up and the 'Dirty Look'. The 'Dirty Look' computer is checking for fraud.

Now the reassuring voice at the end of the line will tell you to replace the telephone and expect a call back. You are climbing the Camelot tree.

Twenty minutes later the phone rings and someone from Camelot's public affairs department comes on the line. Again the voice is reassuring, even more friendly this time. Names are exchanged so that the trembling winner at last feels something tangible is happening. By now Camelot will have a fair idea of the size of your jackpot win.

'We think you have won £22.5 million,' the voice might say.

As you drop your glass of brown ale on the new living-room carpet, paid for on the bank overdraft, the adviser will stress the importance of keeping your win secret for the moment, until you are absolutely sure you want the world to share your joy – and that you are certain you can cope with the publicity. They will want to know who you have told so far. If too many people already know, then it will be too late to keep it all quiet because someone will probably tell the Press.

On Sunday, an adviser, trained to hold your hand through this emotional time, will appear on your doorstep – or meet you at a secret destination. He will already have made contact, probably over his mobile telephone that morning as he speeds up a motorway to your town. At this point you will have been informed of the exact size of your jackpot win.

'The big winner is often confused, frightened, mixed up and excited all at once,' a Camelot insider told me. 'This mood manifests itself by unexplainable bouts of laughter or even complete silence. When I finally walk through their front door they realise their win is really real. Some of them have little recollection of the first hour of their win. They have never met a public relations man before, never expected to. They expected a man in a pinstripe suit, instead it's a man from Camelot in his Sunday casuals – jeans, open-necked denim shirt and all that.'

The adviser will do his utmost to put the big winner at ease, suggesting they all have a cup of tea.

'It's important to keep people talking, move the sugar bowl around. Sometimes the big winner invited the family round without telling them why.

'One daughter came running through the front door thinking her father had died because her mother had shouted down the telephone to get here quick!'

The adviser's job is to make Sunday morning a pleasurable experience for the winning family.

Then there is some paperwork to do and the adviser will discuss with the family the merits of holding a press conference, especially if there are any skeletons in the cupboard that may come out later. Always remember that friends and relatives you may not have seen for years will suddenly want to know you again. If you dismiss them out of hand, they could recall something over a pint or two with a reporter in the Rose and Crown.

If that is the case, it may be better to front up the world with the Camelot advisers who will steer you through the excitement and barrage of reporters' questions.

Keeping your win quiet is difficult. Depositing a cheque for £22.5 million at your local bank will raise a few eyebrows. And there's no doubt that the cheque is from the National Lottery either. It has the symbolic blue fingers on it.

'There are ways around this, though,' says the Camelot insider. 'We can approach the Chief Executive's office at the bank's headquarters and arrange for the cheque to be handled there. Similarly, we can approach the bosses of certain tour firms to fly you away with the minimum of fuss and the maximum of secrecy.'

The adviser is at your beck and call all weekend. But before he leaves you for an hour to check into a near-by hotel, he gives you something you never expected . . . the little Camelot 'Bible'.

'When the winner flicks through the pages of the document *Out of the Blue – It's You!* he or she feels they have something physical, something real. It must be them after all.'

The booklet features a huge, smiling cartoon face on the cover. When you open it up there is a letter of congratulations from Camelot's Chief Executive, Tim Holley.

'You are probably wondering when your feet are going to touch the ground again,' he says. 'You may be asking yourself, "What should I do immediately? What effect could my win have on my life style, my plans for the future? How much should I invest and how? Will there be media publicity and how will I cope with it? What about tax or legal implications? Do I need professional advice? If so, what kind?"

'These are all very natural and important questions. The aim of this document is not to provide you with instant, ready-made answers because there aren't any. What you do with your winnings has to be tailored to your needs, to making your dreams come true.'

The booklet steers the big winner through the minefield of publicity and investment and features boxes for you to fill in such as DAYDREAMS. There are apparently eight: moving to a new neighbourhood; buying a holiday home in sunny Spain or a cottage in the English countryside; a new car with all the luxury trimmings; a trip round the world; flying lessons; golf club membership; a swimming pool in the garden; or a donation to your favourite charity.

There are two columns in the right-hand side for you to fill in: COST and WHEN? Another box is simply entitled NEEDS. Again eight are highlighted: a new home; improvements to your existing home; new furniture or household appliances; higher retirement income; increased regular income now; more money in the bank in case of emergencies; paying off the mortgage and debts; financial security for members of your immediate family. Again there are two columns on the right for you to fill in: COST and WHEN?

The booklet even gives advice on how to deal with reporters.

'They will want to know such things as how you feel about your win,' it says. 'How it might change your life, how you intend to spend the money, and so forth. You will probably be asked to pose for pictures with your partner and your children.

'Remember that your win is a happy story. That's how reporters will generally want to write it up and it will brighten a lot of breakfast tables.

'When you are asked for an interview, ask what sort of questions are likely to be put to you; how long the interview and/or photography will last; and when, where and how it will take place. If you don't like or can't manage what is proposed, say so and fix alternative arrangements. Avoid being rushed into questions. Take your time, and if there are any questions you would prefer not to answer, tell the reporter.'

Finally, the document featuring a cartoon character dreaming about yachts, golf and big houses, advises the big winner not to feel pressurised.

'You are in control,' it says. 'Do things your own way and in your own time. What you need at this stage is just to think over the options for using your money, including both spending on yourself and any gifts to others.'

As an adviser prepares to leave your front room, he will ask the all-important question, 'When would you like to pick up the cheque?'

'Some people are absolutely stunned by this question,' says the Camelot insider. 'They don't expect it to be so easy. When you tell them they can have it on Monday they stare at each other in almost disbelief. Then of course a great debate ensues about where to pick up the money. And they don't always choose to go to the nearest Camelot office.

'They would rather go to Leeds even though Manchester is nearer, because of road works they had been told about on the motorway.'

Finally the moment you have been waiting for arrives – the cheque is handed over to you with the minimum of fuss.

But if you have decided to tell the world about your good fortune, you may be invited to appear on the *National Lottery Live* TV programme when a celebrity will beam in front of the cameras and hand you a cheque the size of your front door.

'Remember,' says the Camelot insider, 'keeping your big win quiet involves a certain amount of lying . . . telling fibs about how you could afford the new Jaguar, fibs to your children about the exotic holiday they are going on, just in case they tell schoolfriends about your good fortune.'

The following week, after you have had time to digest your win, the Camelot panel is at your beck and call and you will be offered legal and financial advice. But you don't have to take it. If you scoop a mega jackpot they will be around for you to consult for up to five years after your win.

Most of the begging letters arrive addressed to the winner at a Camelot office. It is up to you whether you want to see them. If not, Camelot will take care of it all. In most cases the letters are from charities and relatives. Some are simply addressed to Fred Bloggs, Lottery winner, Blackburn.

Says Camelot's Louise White, 'We just want our winners to have fun, and that is why we are really on hand to help them.'

For anyone winning one of the big roll-over prizes the money can lead to as much pain as paradise, and lives can be changed in ways that are not always expected or welcome. Former lovers, ex-wives, illegitimate babies and disgruntled work colleagues will soon be chasing your tail.

That's why Camelot provides the team of experts to help the newly-rich come to terms with their windfall, as they begin to realise they are as famous as the last millionaire lottery winner's Ferrari Testarossa.

The jackpot winner is introduced to a lawyer, an accountant and an investment adviser, and even offered the services of a counsellor. Says Camelot director David Rigg, 'The first thing we advise our winners to do is to wait at least a week before making any major spending plans. It is important to calm down, get used to the idea that they can now have anything they want – as long as it can be bought! The last thing anyone should do is to embark on a completely different life style, because that can be very hard to handle.'

One Camelot worker whose job is to help the big winners through the early weeks of the windfall, says, 'Hitting the jackpot comes as an enormous shock. The winning family is invariably confused, perplexed, unable to grasp what has happened. The mega winners can hardly speak, drink or eat and they lose pounds in weight between Saturday night and Tuesday when they finally bank the cheque. They go through periods of sheer elation, followed by long hours of depression. Many can't sleep, eat, or think straight – and they are highly vulnerable to people who want to part them from their cash. Think about it. We all dream of winning £22.5 million and what we would do with the money. But when the dream becomes reality, handling the reality is hard. You don't trust your dreams any more. Suddenly you believe you have to be sensible. Although you have spent the money in your mind, spending it in reality is another game. You are suddenly far richer than the hack from Camelot standing in the room with you. You are suddenly as famous as Cliff Richard, and really you never expected to be.'

Camelot's special team will show you how to give money to relatives without handing most of it to the taxman and help you deal with the begging letters and telephone calls that can turn winning into a nightmare. The ideal solution is, of course, to tell no one and gradually and quietly get used to the money. But that can be almost impossible. One early million-plus winner's identity was let slip by his six-year-old grandson when he told his friends at school. Another kept mum, but had to come clean after splashing out on a new car – a suspicious neighbour called the police, tipping them off that he had robbed a local building society. One big winner's answer was to buy round-the-world tickets for himself, his wife and kids. They haven't been seen since. 'He's perfectly happy and sends us great-to-be-here postcards from the most exotic places on earth,' said a Camelot spokesman. 'Winning the money should make people happy and that's what we want to hear!'

Meanwhile lottery winners who can't cope with the strain of becoming millionaires are given special counselling under a Camelot 'Coming Out' programme designed to help winners go public gradually. The scheme involves them being presented to their local media a month or so after winning the jackpot.

'Saying you are buying a new car or house because

you have come into some money from an aunt in Australia is a story you can only maintain for a while,' said communications director David Rigg. 'It is clear some people are finding a lie very difficult to cope with.'

His Camelot colleague Louise White added, 'Part of winning a large amount of money is sharing that news with people and getting it off your chest.'

Since the lottery began, twenty-five million of us have dared to wonder, 'Could it be me?' Almost half the population is delirious with greed, we have gone lotto blotto, intoxicated by dreams of avarice. We stand in the supermarket queue muttering about new cars, yachts, country houses and paying off the mortgage.

We know the dismal odds. The ratio of fourteen million to one is tattooed on the part of our brain that stores disagreeable information, but that is no deterrent. We are lured on by the smiling faces of new-age millionaires staring out of the pages of the national newspapers.

But if we really did win the big one, what should we do with all that lovely lolly?

The Abbey National Building Society calculates that £22.5 million would earn £4,666 a day in interest. That is £32,668 a week or £1,698,750 a year. There would be a forty per cent tax bill on the interest, because the winner would automatically become a higher rate taxpayer. The basic rate tax would be deducted from the building society accounts, but at the end of the year the Inland Revenue would demand another fifteen per cent.

Whatever you do, the prize will bring a big income and a big tax bill. Tax breaks are irrelevant on such a vast amount so don't worry about putting a few thousand into PEPs and TESSAs. If you resent handing over big chunks to the taxman, go and live in the Isle of Man or Monte Carlo.

The most important thing is not to rush into anything. Draw out £100,000 for a few instant treats, then take your time. Next, pay off all your debts and put five per cent into a charitable trust to give away. You will be pestered by begging letters and this will deal with the problem and be good for your conscience.

Put another five per cent away and have fun with it – parties, holidays, cars and so on.

Naturally, you will need good financial advisers.

If you were lucky enough to win £22.5 million you really would never have to worry about the money running out. You would be able to employ the most private bankers and the poshest stockbrokers like Cazenoves, who look after the Royal Family. Your £22.5 million is probably more liquid cash than the Queen could lay her hands on.

So draw up a list of well-known names and ask them to submit their recommendations. The advisers will probably suggest setting up an off-shore family fund with a group of trustees to decide where to invest. They would probably put forty per cent into government gilts and the other sixty per cent into shares. Don't worry about investing in art or wine. Just buy a few bottles or paintings out of your blow money.

Don't try to change your life style dramatically. It is

essential if you live in a council flat that you don't move to a house in Belgravia or Ascot. The dramatic change of environment and culture could lead to depression. If you drink pints of bitter every night, dine on takeaways and smoke roll-ups, the champagne set may snub you. So the last thing you want to do is go and live alongside them.

Giving up work can leave you bored and dissatisfied. But think carefully about a new career. Many people say they would love to run a pub, but you would have to work seven days a week, 365 days a year. Why do that when you don't have to?

One of the first National Lottery winners scooped £839,254. Britain clapped and cheered. Then along came the first roll-over jackpot man, Mukhtar Mohidin. The hard-working husband and father visibly shook the night he realised he had won £17.8 million. Good news for Camelot, or so they thought.

Mukhtar was Britain's biggest prize winner ever. Yet, even with his £17.8 million National Lottery jackpot, he was still only 1,500th in the table of the UK's richest people, just behind the Queen Mother at £18 million, and Noel Edmonds at £19 million.

Mukhtar's new-found buying power was simply not in the same league as that of Jack Walker, the boss of his favourite team, Blackburn Rovers. He splashed out more than £29 million of his personal £320 million fortune on his slavish devotion to football. This enabled manager Kenny Dalglish to buy little treats like goalkeeper Tim Flowers (£2 million), midfield player David Batty (£2.75 million) and strikers Paul Warhurst (£2.7 million), Alan Shearer (£3.3 million) and the £5 million man Chris Sutton. The spree may have taken the team to the top of the Premiership League, but such a shopping list would have left Mukhtar deep in debt again.

So if, like Mukhtar, you were to win £17.8 million, what could you afford to buy?

For a start, a more affordable option would be to forget football and, like billionaire John Paul Getty, become obsessed with cricket instead. Since being introduced to the game's intricacies by rock legend Mick Jagger, the American-born philanthropist has given £3 million for a stand at Lord's and has also had a cricket pitch laid at a cost of around £500,000, complete with mock-Tudor pavilion and a thatched score-box at Wormsley, his 3,000-acre Buckinghamshire estate. But would you be able to buy such a lavish country seat in the first place and still have change? Most probably not.

There's simply no way, for instance, that your funds would stretch to the £30 million California ranch where Michael Jackson lives and where Liz Taylor staged her most recent marriage. It boasts a £1.5 million games room and a £90,000 oxygen chamber in which Jackson sleeps. The electricity bill for the security searchlights around his home is around £20,000 a month.

Jackson is also reported to spend £150,000 a year on flowers and £50,000 a month on designer clothes for his chimps, Alexandria and Max. In fifteen years, he has splashed out £190,000 on plastic surgery (surely a sound investment, if you are a lottery winner wishing to avoid irate friends, family or religious leaders).

No, you would have to settle for a more modest

dwelling, perhaps something like the three apart-
ments on the thirty-sixth floor of an Atlanta tower
block which Elton John bought for £3 million. He then
lavished a further £4 million knocking them together
and filled them with artworks and furnishings, which
included a £70,000, hand-crafted bed, commissioned
from royal furniture-maker Viscount Linley, naturally. Elton went on to pay out a further £1 million
renovating and decorating a £180,000 home near-by
as a guesthouse for his friends – but if, as many
winners seem to, you had fallen out with many of
yours, you would be spared this extra expense.

Once you have settled into your new home, a
sensible way to fill it could be to buy works of art,
which might some day be worth millions. But be
careful. Ask yourself whether you really know anything about Canaletto and Rubens and the rest.

Composer Andrew Lloyd Webber added to his vast
private art collection when he purchased a £10 million
painting, 'The Old Horseguards' by Canaletto. Lloyd
Webber, whose fortune is estimated at £300 million,
spent more on that one painting than on his ex-wife
Sarah Brightman. He only gave her a £6 million
divorce settlement.

Madonna meanwhile paid a more modest £1 million
for a Picasso and has an extensive collection of valuable Art Deco. But beware; *Rocky* star Sylvester
Stallone reportedly blew £50 million on bad art investments and is currently selling works which he painted
himself for around £20,000 a time.

If you really want a new car, how about a McLaren
FI for £540,000, a Bentley Azure at £215,000 or a
Lamborghini Diablo, a snip at £143,932. Or, like

guitarist Eric Clapton, you might consider becoming a Ferrari fanatic. The latest model, the 456, sells at £151,750.

After all the hard work of spending you would probably need a holiday. Why not then, embark on a forty-two-day trip across two continents, like Viscount Linley and his bride on their honeymoon? Their romantic adventure took in Harare; Camp Amalinda in Bulawayo; the Tongabezi Camp in Zambia; Livingstone and Victoria Falls; a two-week, landcruiser safari in Botswana; a stopover in Johannesburg; and a two-and-a-half week tour of the USA and Canada.

One travel agent worked out that even flying economy class and sharing middle-range hotel rooms (which is doubtful) this would have cost at least £13,000 in flights and hotels alone – not counting the couple's week at Princess Margaret's holiday home in Mustique.

You could hire a luxury yacht. The 170-foot *Lady Mona K*, once owned by the late publisher Robert Maxwell as *Lady Ghislaine*, can be chartered for around £120,000 a week, excluding fuel, food and drink. But be sure to take swimming lessons first.

If you do want to do some serious shopping on your holiday, why not book into the Imperial Suite at the Hotel Ritz in Paris. A night will cost you around £615 (49,620FF) in high season. Once there you could treat yourself to a pair of Cartier spectacles, bedecked with diamonds, rubies, sapphires and emeralds (£70,000) or a crocodile handbag with a gem-set clasp (£65,000) and invest in a suit from Chanel couture for around £10,000. But don't overdo things as the spendthrift king, boxer Mike

Tyson, did. The ex-world champion blew £42 million in three years – and couldn't remember where it had gone. Before being jailed for rape and becoming a Muslim, he had thirty cars, including Rolls-Royces, Bentleys, Ferraris and Mercedes and bought mansions, furs and expensive jewellery.

Alternatively, if cars weren't your bag, you could travel to New York and back on Concorde 4,000 times.

So, as you can see, Mukhtar and other lottery winners sadly had no chance of truly tasting the life of the seriously rich and famous.

If you were to win somewhere in the region of £1 million, before you even consider spending a penny of it, bank the lot. Then celebrate and get some good advice, preferably before you have thrown in your job and planned an eighteen-hole golf course for the garden.

John Mitchell, managing director of stockbrokers Tilney and Co., is a member of the independent panel that offers financial advice to the big Littlewoods Pools' winners. The panel was set up in the wake of Vivian Nicholson's 'spend, spend, spend' era. What would his advice be to a new millionaire?

'They've had all the luck they are ever likely to get and the last thing they want is further risk,' he says. 'They should play safe and sleep at night.'

Handling a windfall of this size is as much an emotional and psychological matter as a practical one, John says. 'Part of our job is education, explaining to someone just what the money can and cannot do. For example, you might get a £300,000 winner who wants to buy a house and a BMW and quit his job. But you

41

have to explain there wouldn't be enough left to live on. Or someone might win £2 million and have no appreciation of how much that is.'

The first stage is to assess your expectations, he adds. Do you want to move home, give up work, go on a cruise? What are your spending plans?

'Generally they are very modest. People don't really want a gold Rolls-Royce. If they have got a three-bedroom council house they want a four-bedroom house around the corner – but they want to own it. They want to keep their friends and that is sensible. Some see the money as all theirs, others want to share it. One million-pound winner split the money and gave half away, but got through his share in three months and came back for more. So we try to talk them out of that sort of thing.'

Leaks and gossip are the reason many winners go public. Secrecy can be restrictive. John recalls one young man who didn't want to tell anyone about his good fortune but he wanted to buy a red Ferrari and park it outside his front door.

Investing the nest egg is where the safety-first approach comes in.

'A Pools winner has already cracked the big gamble of his or her life,' says John. 'He or she doesn't want a racy portfolio. But just sticking money in the bank is the biggest risk of all because inflation can knock it for six.'

Generally, advisers tend to recommend a combination of equities and index-linked government stocks to provide both income and growth of capital. On the whole they counsel against business ventures.

'Thinking you would like to own a restaurant when

you know nothing about owning restaurants can be a recipe for disaster,' John says. 'It's different if you've worked in a pub for thirty years and always dreamed of having your own.'

Property is no longer regarded as the fail-safe investment it once was. Michael Critchley, a manager with Barclays Bank, who helped advise the first £1 million Premium Bond winner, says, 'You should buy a house you are happy living in rather than thinking of it as a way of making money, because it can turn out to be a burden.'

Similarly, he believes that jewellery, works of art, antiques and others luxuries should be bought for pleasure rather than financial gain.

After the initial indulgences, winners should put away 'rainy day' money: cash to hand if the roof blows off or they want a spur of the moment holiday. Longer-term investment should be in blue chip companies and gilts.

'It may be important psychologically to blow a bit of the money, but once things have cooled down you should remember this is a once in a lifetime chance,' Michael says.

Gamblers hoping to scoop the lottery jackpot will be encouraged by the knowledge that, in Michael's experience, money can bring happiness.

'You do get disasters,' he says, 'but most people are as happy as Larry for the rest of their lives.'

Most of us of course, will never win the lottery, even though we think we will. But what do we really plan to do with all the money we are never going to have?

One survey from Barclays attempted to find the answer.

It asked the simple question: What would be the first thing you did if you won the National Lottery? Forty-five per cent of all women questioned said they would treat close family and friends. Thirty-three per cent of males thought the same.

Thirty-three per cent of men wanted to invest most or all of the windfall. Only twenty-four per cent of women agreed.

Just a small percentage of both sexes would pay off their bills, the mortgage, credit cards and loans: eighteen per cent of men and nineteen per cent of the women. And strangely, only eight per cent of the women would splash out on a new wardrobe, a new car or luxury holiday. For men the figure was higher – eleven per cent.

Although three out of four people in Britain were gambling on the National Lottery, ninety-two per cent of them were still saving, the survey revealed. A higher proportion of women were playing, but men were spending more on tickets. One in five men spent between £5 and £10 each week compared to one in twelve women.

Devon and Cornwall seemed to be the most caring places. Fifty-six per cent of those questioned would treat family and friends from their win. In Yorkshire the figure was thirty-three per cent. People in the recession-hit south-east and London were more eager to clear their debts: twenty-six per cent would pay them up. In Devon and Cornwall the figure was just three per cent.

Barclays' profile of the average lottery player was a

fifty-five-year-old woman in full-time employment, living in London or the south-east, gambling £2 to £4 a week.

Another survey revealed that only two in five people would immediately walk out of their jobs and retire if they won the lottery.

Chapter Three

Mukhtar's in the Money!

It was hard work as a packer at the Blythe Chemicals factory but worth it. Mukhtar Mohidin smiled as he walked down the path and looked at the fruits of his labours – a smart, three-bedroomed, semi-detached house on the estate of prestigious Barratt Homes.

He was proud of his little castle which had cost him £49,950 and particularly proud of the £5,000 conservatory he had added to it at the back. But he was tired because he had just finished the night shift. Little did he know that within days he would never have to return to work and his life would change so radically that he would never shop at his local Tesco store again.

In December 1994, forty-two-year-old Mukhtar and his wife Sayeeda, thirty-two, scooped the £17.8 million National Lottery jackpot. That day was a turning point for him and his family and gave birth to the rows that would begin to mar a game that was launched to bring fun to a nation and millions of pounds for charity. The writs would soon be flying. Camelot would soon be smarting.

For Mukhtar life would be difficult. In his mind he had often gone over what to do with the money if he won. But in his wildest dreams he never imagined the blaze of publicity, the family arguments, the religious recriminations, the enormous spending power that would follow. Mukhtar was never able to sit back and take time to think about his win as the private Camelot brochure for lottery millionaires advises. He never had a chance from the start. From the moment a man from Camelot helped the mixed-up winner to scramble over his back-garden fence to escape the Press . . . to the day some members of his own mosque snubbed him, his place in the history books was sealed.

Until that day it had been a long, hard graft for the couple who had devoted their whole lives to doing the best for their three sons.

Mukhtar was the son of Indian immigrants in Tanzania. He left Africa in the late 1970s to join his brother Majid in Blackburn. Soon he entered into an arranged marriage with a pretty, nineteen-year-old girl named Sayeeda. The newly-weds bought a small, terraced house in Little Harwood, a district of Blackburn, and took a mortgage on a rundown corner shop.

Mukhtar was ambitious. He spent thousands of pounds doing up the shop – with a master plan to rent it out. But for a while work came to a halt when he ran out of money.

For years he slaved in factory jobs never daring to refuse extra shifts or a few hours' overtime because he desperately needed the money to fulfil his dreams.

Finally he found a tenant for the shop and he breathed a sigh of relief. But things didn't turn out the way he expected and the business later moved. Sadly, Mukhtar had the shop boarded up.

His wife Sayeeda was supportive. As well as running the home and raising their three sons, she took a job as a machinist in a shoe factory to help provide the extra cash for her boys, aged six, eight and twelve.

Friends regarded Mukhtar as a workaholic who was always ready to boost his £250-a-week earnings. His simple pleasures in life were supporting Blackburn Rovers and a weekly flutter on the Pools. His typical rota was seven nights a week from 9.30p.m. to 6a.m.; seven afternoons from 1.30p.m. to 9.30p.m. Then he would have a day off before seven shifts from 6a.m. to 1.30p.m. All the hard work paid off when in October 1994 the proud family moved into their smart three-bedroomed semi.

The Mohidins adopted Western customs and dress. Mukhtar and Sayeeda wore jeans and sweaters, although she still had traditional clothes for Muslim ceremonies.

The family had broad Lancashire accents and Mukhtar, a keen handyman, was often seen outside his house tinkering with his old E-registered Datsun. Neighbours said the couple were very nice and friendly and the children were always smartly turned out.

As a Muslim, Mukhtar did not drink, and he worshipped at the Masjid al Momineen mosque in Ash Street, Blackburn. He was a great cook – known at the chemical plant as the Curry King.

'He used to bring in curries and heat them up on a

little cooker in our mess cabin. They were delicious,'
said a workmate.

Like most families, once a week the Mohidins would
go shopping together. In fact their trips to town were
a bit of a joke among family and friends and led to
gentle teasing because of their quiet and sober life
style.

'That was the highlight of their week,' a relative
confessed.

It was on one such trip that Mukhtar decided to call
into Tesco's for a lottery ticket in defiance of his
religion's ban on gambling.

'We were all given sermons at the mosque that
games of chance were forbidden, but a lot of us were
tempted,' said a friend who met Mukhtar on his way
to the fateful purchase.

'He told me he was popping in to the store to buy
lottery tickets. Then I learned he had won.'

That win turned Mukhtar's life upside down. For two
days the world's media was on his tail and the *Sun*
newspaper was closing in. As he was originally identified by Camelot not by name, but only as an Asian
factory worker who enjoyed cooking curries, some tabloid newspapers nicknamed him Mr Vindaloot.

'Mukhtar had a touching faith that his family and
friends would never reveal his identity,' said a lottery
insider. 'In fact, to be fair to them, his close family
never did.'

Finally the man from Camelot was receiving messages from his aides over his mobile telephone in
Mukhtar's front room. They were telling him about
the reporters and photographers getting nearer. 'It's
the Currant Bun (*Sun*), they're in town,' one message

said. An hour later, 'They're only about half a mile
away.'

The Camelot man looked out of the front window
when the voice finally said, 'They're about 200 yards
from you.'

The adviser pushed Mukhtar out of the back door and
they scaled the six-foot garden fence together, as the
reporters walked up the front path. Mukhtar went into
hiding at his mother's house as the Camelot man
returned to get his suitcase. Now the rear of the neat
semi-detached was covered by the *Sun . . .* and the
reporters recognised him – he was a former Fleet Street
hack. For weeks he would be pestered for Mukhtar's
name and new address but he never handed it over.

Mukhtar fled to his sister's London home, then
went off under cover to a hideaway in the Indian
Ocean, after Camelot got him special clearance at
Gatwick. Before he left he confessed to a friend, 'I've
never known anything like this. I've been chain
smoking ever since I won. Perhaps I'll go to a country
like America.'

America wasn't a good idea. For under the freedom
of information act, the names of lottery winners were
always revealed and that was the last thing Mukhtar
wanted. US organisers, along with Camelot, believed
publicity helped sell tickets and that in turn brought
more money into the good causes they backed.

Mukhtar's first attempts to spend his fortune failed.
He really tried hard to put things right. But the man
who won £17.8 million found he couldn't even give his
money away. Fellow Muslims snubbed his plans
because their religion forbade gambling. They
branded the money 'tainted' and accused Mukhtar of

setting a bad example. Why then did he do it after seemingly believing so much in his religion? Mixed-up Mukhtar at this point was trying to please everyone, said a lottery insider. 'But everything he did seemed to go wrong. Deep inside, you see, he was a very religious person. Now a conflict was going on but the Press never reflected that.'

Close friends said he wanted to give at least £1 million to the Islamic Relief Charity and £200,000 for the building of a community centre next to the Masjid al Momineen mosque. His attempts were thwarted.

Islamic Relief accused him of setting a bad example to Muslims by defying strict rules on gambling in the Koran, the Muslims' holy book.

Fund-raiser Ashfaq Burondkar said, 'He has done wrong. There is no pleasure in a donation like this. We cannot accept it. This win is terrible because it will encourage all Muslims to gamble and that is wrong because it damages families. There is already one case of a man divorcing his wife in Blackburn because he only got two winning numbers and he blamed her.'

The prospect of a donation to the mosque arose on a chilly, winter Sunday evening when members met in their main hall. It was the day after Mukhtar's jackpot win. They discussed the financing of a £200,000 community centre and as they argued about how they could possibly pay for it, one of Mukhtar's relatives told them, 'Don't worry – go ahead. There will be money.'

But treasurer Ibrahim Khan said, 'Neither the mosque nor his family can accept any of the money because it is *haram* – forbidden. If someone makes a donation I must ask where it comes from and if it is from gambling I cannot accept it. Our religion is very hard.'

He added that the man would be 'punished by God' for his sin although he would still be welcome to attend prayers. Another mosque elder said, 'We could not accept any of that money and strictly speaking nor can his family. He can go to the mosque and pray for forgiveness, but that is not a matter for us. It is up to God to forgive him. A Muslim has to answer for himself. We are not here to judge individuals. It is up to his own conscience.'

The leader of Britain's 'Muslim Parliament', Dr Kalim Siddiqui, took issue with the critics. He pointed out that although Muslims should never gamble it was permissible for mosques or charities to accept the proceeds. Some scholars close to Islamic Relief also said it could be accepted as long as it was used purely to help the poor and not for anything sacred such as a mosque.

The debate went on and everyone seemed to have different ideas. A friend of Mukhtar's said, 'Some think it has brought shame to our religion. I don't agree. If Mukhtar gives a large slice to charity, it will become a power for good not evil.'

This, then, was the backcloth to Mukhtar's big win.

Things weren't going smoothly for him. He could do no right. He confided to a close friend, 'People either love me for the money I have won or they hate me. Some think I should give it all away, but would they?'

As the former Blackburn factory worker stayed in hiding with his wife and three children, his best friend, Ismail Lorgat, was consulting his solicitor and preparing for a High Court action to sue him for four-ninths of his fortune. At every turn Mukhtar was losing. Forty-two-year-old Ismail claimed he helped buy the lucky winning ticket and insisted that they had agreed to split the proceeds.

'I can still hear Mukhtar's last words to me just days after the 10 December draw,' he said. 'I managed to get a telephone call through to him and told him I hoped he wouldn't let me down.

'He replied, "Don't worry, I'll see you right!" Since then I've waited and waited hoping he'd get in touch. I feel very bitter and unhappy.

'At first I was a bit fearful for Mukhtar's safety. But then I could only think that he was staying away because he wanted to.'

The two men had known each other for fifteen years, since Mukhtar arrived from East Africa.

'We became very close,' said father-of-four Ismail. 'At one stage I rented the corner shop he owned. Mukhtar popped in daily for a chat. He often came to my allotment and house too. We would talk about cabbages and football. My wife always welcomed him and our kids became playmates.

'We'd even sit for hours over a coffee or Coke talking about money, the day's events and family matters. Then last September I gave him notice from the shop because I needed to expand my upholstery business and the place was too small. He was sad but understood and it didn't affect our friendship.

'Mukhtar brought the final electricity bill for the shop to my house a week before the lottery draw. It was for £46 and some odd pence, I can't remember the exact figure. I gave him £50 in £10 notes. He had no change but I told him to pay it out of the cash I had given him.'

The following Saturday the friends met at Ismail's new furniture factory. Ismail recalled, 'Mukhtar told me he had paid the electricity bill. He had my change but I never got round to taking it.

'He said he was off to Tesco's to do some shopping and buy some lottery tickets. I told him I'd always been a lucky person and he should buy extra lottery tickets with my change.

'He got all serious and said, "If we win we will share it".'

Ismail claimed he told Mukhtar that the odds against winning were so high that the lottery shouldn't be taken seriously. He alleged he used an Asian expression *Dil Behlane* which roughly translates, 'Do it for fun'.

That evening the numbers chosen by Mukhtar won Britain's biggest lottery jackpot since the launch. Next day Ismail heard rumours about his chum's good fortune and he couldn't believe his luck when the win was finally confirmed to him by reporters.

But within days of claiming the prize, Mukhtar, his wife Sayeeda and their three children had left their £50,000 home.

'I was so happy and I couldn't sleep through excitement,' said Ismail. 'I stayed working at my factory into the early hours. I was building castles in the air, dreaming of what I would do with my share. That's when I discovered Mukhtar had left the district.'

Ismail spent days frantically tracing his friend. Finally he found him in London.

The following Sunday all was revealed when the

News of the World published Mukhtar's name and photograph. Since the win, Mukhtar has not been seen back in Blackburn. The workaholic, once known to go a month without taking a day off, never returned.

'I haven't said anything about all this before because my religious leaders gave sermons against the lottery,' said Ismail. 'I do strongly believe in Islamic values. If I won the money I would not keep it. I would have to give it all away.'

Mukhtar's millions may have caused nothing but unhappiness to his friend, but it also caused heartache for his widowed mother and two brothers, none of whom at this time had apparently seen any of the prize money.

Meanwhile welfare officers called at the junior school in Blackburn that Mukhtar's three children attended. They had not been seen since the 10 December draw.

A family friend said, 'I know there has been a terrible family row. The mosque isn't happy and neither is Mukhtar.'

Towards the end of December the winner's distraught family finally managed to make contact with Mukhtar because his elderly mother had fallen ill. He got in touch with her. But soon he faded back into obscurity. Then one day a letter turned up at Blythe Chemicals in Hapton, Lancs, where he had been a packer for sixteen years. He had quit his job as everyone expected.

It was the end of an era for Mukhtar and the end of a dream for Camelot. It had hoped, along with the BBC's *National Lottery Live* producers, to parade a never-ending succession of new millionaires before the cameras. But the flight of 'Mr Vindaloot', whose real name had now been published by some newspapers, put paid to that prospect.

For Mukhtar things went from bad to worse. There was no happiness for the National Lottery punters in the story. Only intrigue. Early in May, he was arrested after a family bust-up over his fortune and spent three hours cooling off in a cell at a police station in Amersham, Buckinghamshire. He had blown his top at a reunion for relatives and friends when they squabbled over who was entitled to a share of his cash. The row grew so fierce that he bundled two male guests into a car and drove them to the police station.

'He felt they just wanted his money and not his love and friendship,' said a lottery insider.

All three were arrested and held until they calmed down, then freed without being charged. A Thames Valley policeman was staggered. He said, 'It's amazing that winning so much money can bring so many problems.'

Mukhtar, it appeared, wasn't a good advertisement for Camelot. Or was he? At least his story kept the lottery in the public eye.

The lucky winner now started a new life in the south of England under a different name. When he was arrested he gave his home address as Blackburn, but told officers he was looking for a mansion in the Home Counties. Today he lives in a £375,000, six-bedroom house, has shaved his head and his children are taught privately, their identity protected by a legal order. Life for them all is beginning to settle down, as it should for every lottery winner.

The bonanza he collected is likely to have made him over £1 million in interest since the fateful day of his win, and he finally declared peace in the family, giving away £2.5 million of his fortune to heal the rifts. There were gifts to brothers, cousins, aunts and uncles and his wife's relations. He was desperately trying to make things right. But he wasn't having the luck he had had picking his jackpot numbers. For more trouble was eventually to follow.

Following talks with his lawyers and advisers, he gave sums from £500,000 to his mother and brothers down to £50,000 to nearly twenty other family members.

A cousin who received £50,000 said, 'The money was causing all sorts of problems. He was angry that people were expecting a handout and he didn't know what to do. He was having difficulty coming to terms with the win and the pressure it was causing. I suppose it was natural that he was suspicious of everyone and their motives and he refused to talk about it all. In the end he thought everyone was trying to take the money from him. Since making the decision to share the winnings, he has gone back to his ordinary, friendly self. It is a load off his mind.'

Mukhtar was obviously wisely advised.

Shortly afterwards he did speak out. 'I'm not spoiling the kids, and my wife and I don't act like millionaires,' he said. 'I still eat curries, but now I can afford better ones. I'm not miserable like people have tried to make out. I'm happy now that I have learned to cope with my fortune.'

But behind the scenes he and Sayeeda were accusing each other of giving away too much money to relatives. Hadn't they read Camelot's millionaire's handbook? Nevertheless Mukhtar had some advice for the latest lottery roll-over winners.

'They must be sensible how they use the money and not be too overwhelmed by it all. I wish them much luck,' he said.

Weeks later luck ran out for Mukhtar's wife Sayeeda. The millionaire was suing her to stop her getting her hands on his £17.8 million jackpot. Why? Because she had started proceedings against him for equal rights to the money. To the Press they astonishingly insisted that all was still sweetness and light.

'They have a touching belief in people,' a Camelot informant, who cannot be named, told me. 'They don't really understand the ways of the media. But they are trying hard.'

Sayeeda declared, 'I am living happily with my husband and family and have no reason to expect that this happy state of affairs will not continue.'

But the writs were a testament to the bitterness and jealousy which had dogged the pair since their win. Sayeeda was suing under the Married Woman's Property Act for joint ownership of the jackpot. In response Mukhtar filed a writ asking the courts to rule that he was not bound by an authority he signed in May which allowed his wife to take money from an account held at the Yorkshire Bank plc. He also sought a declaration that he was 'solely and beneficially' entitled to the money he won. Mukhtar would also be seeking costs if he won.

Behind the scenes Mukhtar was apparently trying

to stop his wife giving cash to 'droves of her relatives'. Sayeeda was reportedly arguing that her husband was now being 'too generous' to his relations.

In his statement, Mukhtar said, 'I bought the tickets from my own money. The prize money was, and remains, mine – absolutely in every sense!'

Devoted Sayeeda said, 'We are still very much in love. I have no plans to move out and neither has he. What my husband and I do about the money is our business.'

Soon after Mukhtar's huge win it was revealed that most National Lottery players wanted a limit on the size of payouts. A maximum £5 million top prize would be ideal, according to one survey. Punters wanted the extra money to be used to boost wins for four and five correct numbers.

The survey carried out for the TSB Bank indicated that people felt large sums like Mukhtar's £17.8 million were just too big. Was it envy?

Of nearly 1,000 people questioned for the TSB by the leading pollsters, NOP, fifty-four per cent said there should be a maximum big win. Only twenty-six per cent thought there should be no upper limit and three-quarters wanted improved smaller prizes. This echoed the views of the Archbishop of Canterbury, who attacked the monster jackpots as offering false hopes and over-indulgence.

Richard Branson, who failed in his bid to run the lottery, announced, 'I don't want to sound like a bad loser but if we had won instead of Camelot, there would be seven guaranteed millionaires a week with a maximum win of £6 million. I think the public would prefer 365 new millionaires a year rather than a small number of mega-millionaires.'

John Major also said that jackpots might be too large, especially after several multi-million-pound wins. The Cabinet was aware of the widespread concern at the sizes of the top prizes, but Mr Major refused to intervene to cap the mega payouts, although he failed to rule out introducing tighter restrictions in the future.

MPs, the Church and charities had attacked the roll-over jackpots, claiming people had problems handling wealth and fame.

In a Britain struggling to rise again like the sleeping lion, to find its identity, to discover hope and a way forward, the lottery had become a Pandora's box.

As we queue for our lottery tickets we are all searching for a quality of life that we have come to expect. But remember, when Merlin spins out the numbers, it could be you, but it probably won't be. And winning millions of pounds will not make you a better or more caring person.

Vivian Nicholson turned out to be the best – or possibly the worst – advertisement for winning a fortune. Today she has a message for Camelot – 'For God's sake look after your winners!'

In 1961 Vivian, then twenty-three, worked in a Liquorice Allsorts factory as a £3-a-week Pomfret Cake squasher. She and her twenty-year-old second husband Keith, a £7-a-week trainee miner, won £152,000 on the Football Pools, the equivalent of around £2 million today. The cameras rolled and reporters scribbled in their notebooks as TV star

Bruce Forsyth handed Viv and Keith the cheque that stunned a nation.

'And what are you going to do with it, luv?' Bruce asked.

'I'm going to spend, spend, spend!'

Those words were to be engraved in the annals of media history for ever. But nobody heard Vivian add under her breath, 'We've had the good, now what about the bad?' And she meant it. She had vowed at the age of six to be famous one day – and now she was. Four years later they proved to be prophetic words. Immediately after their win Viv and Keith and their four children left their council home for a vast luxury bungalow in near-by Garforth – and they both gave up their jobs.

'You have to move to a big house because your old neighbours hate thinking of you having pots of money,' said Viv. 'But when you get to a posh new street, your new neighbours hate you for not having to work like they did to get their bungalows. So lottery winners beware.'

The rambling dream home was so big, Viv used to joke that she got lost in it. She put a five-seater leather sofa in the lounge and a massive table in the dining room.

'It was a huge place and took some flippin' filling,' she said.

In fact it wasn't really her at all. She spent most of her time in the kitchen because it was the smallest room in the bungalow and the only place she felt at home in.

There were mammoth boozing sessions, parties around the world and mega bets on the horses, roulette wheels and card tables. More money went on cars – Viv got through eleven in four years, and she would dye her hair to match their colours. Keith had just two. Champagne baths and designer clothes followed. On one shopping trip she bought seven pairs of shoes, one pair for each day of the week, with seven matching outfits. Then on 31 October 1965, Keith died in a car crash. Viv was devastated. But three more husbands and a lot more spending followed. Two of those husbands later died.

Today Viv, now fifty-six, is a devout Jehovah's Witness who lives in a modest terraced house in Castleford, West Yorkshire, a stone's throw from the council home she had when she first married. Now she is reflective and a lot more serious.

'The moment we won £152,000 I knew something was going to happen to Keith and I,' she says. 'We both hated our jobs and couldn't give them up fast enough. I boasted that I could go out and buy fourteen pairs of shoes and book a holiday around the world – and I did. But it didn't compensate for lost peace of mind. I was so mixed up that if I went to the races I would buy two dresses so that on the day I would have a choice.

'Keith and I drank ourselves silly. We would go to the pub at ten in the morning and leave at four in the afternoon. By seven we would be back, staying until four in the morning. The house would be full of drink too. We had wild parties for people we didn't even know, just to have someone in the house we could talk to. People hang around you, hoping for handouts. You need to become a good judge of character very quickly or they will fleece you out of every penny. Our days were becoming long and empty.'

Now Vivian works part-time as a shop assistant and earns well under £100 a week. She wears a uniform and a name badge, just in case there is any doubt about her identity. Customers still can't believe she is hard up. She vows to work as long as she can and admitted, 'Keith and I may have hated our jobs but what we didn't realise was that work, no matter how much you moan about it, gives you a purpose in life. It helps you fill your days and make friends. I got to the point where I wandered aimlessly around the garden or drifted into town to buy yet another pair of shoes until no more would fit in my wardrobe. I even bought expensive jewellery to relieve the boredom. But nothing made my day. Keith bought racehorses and guns to go shooting with our new, posh, so-called friends. We held parties that went on for days. I drank buckets of booze and went on fabulous holidays. Then Keith was killed in a car crash. I'll never forget that day, I think about it all the time. He was the only man I ever loved. For a long time I couldn't forgive him for dying on me. I was hurt. I thought I had been cheated. I remarried to try to prove that I didn't care.'

The money and Keith's death, the drink and the drugs affected Vivian profoundly. One night she was so fed up with all her kids that she drove them to Keith's graveside and left them there for an hour. In her mind she felt they had been nasty to her. So she asked them, 'Who loves Daddy?' They all said they did. So she took them to the cemetery at midnight and listened to them crying. She wanted them to suffer as much as she was suffering.

Vivian's third marriage, to car salesman Graham

Ellison, lasted six months before they split. The fourth ended when husband Brian Wright, a nightclub bouncer, died in a car crash. The fifth, to Gary Shaw in 1972, was over seven weeks later when he took a drugs overdose. He was buried beside her beloved Keith.

Market stallholder, Bernard Curran, almost became her sixth, but Viv got cold feet and jilted him on the day they were to be wed at Pontefract Register Office. He now runs a pub called the Coronation Street and they are still friends. By the time of the wedding that never was, the money had long since run out.

'I drank a bottle of brandy a night. I took drugs and tried to kill myself twice,' says Viv. 'It was all a cry for help – but there was no one there. I had lost all my real friends after winning the Pools. I had gone from being a jovial woman to the loneliest person in the world.'

In 1979 Vivian joined the Jehovah's Witnesses and claims they were her salvation. She now attends Bible meetings five times a week and spends hours door-to-door canvassing.

'I get up early, at about 6.30a.m., but only since I became a Witness,' she says. 'Before then I could drink six or seven bottles of beer, come home, take a couple of tablets, drink a bottle of wine and not surface until four in the afternoon. I was very unhealthy and weighed about seven stone. It was a hard living. Now, after I have said my blessings, and prayed to God to protect me for a brand new day, I get up, go downstairs and boil the kettle for tea. I like Earl Grey, no milk and no sugar. That's to keep the hips down. They ballooned when I gave up smoking years ago. Then out comes my copy of the latest *Watchtower* and I study it, picking out the main points of each article, purely for discussion purposes. When we get together as a group we never argue. I mean you can't dispute what is in the Bible. On the days I am not working, I go out on the services, calling from door to door. It's a field ministry. They are a mixed bunch of people around here. But mostly they are very nice. I can only remember being rebuffed once, which really hurt. It was many years ago. A lady came to the door who'd had a recent bereavement. She had lost her father. I said, "Don't worry, Jehovah will return him." She said, "You can talk – how many husbands have you had back?" I suppose she was reacting to the bad profile the Press has given me over the years.'

Vivian has three sons and a daughter – Stephen by her first husband, miner Matthew Johnson, Sue, Tim and Howard by Keith. She also has six grandchildren.

'The children have their own places,' she says. 'We put money in trust for the youngest three, though mind you, it's spent now. In spite of people writing that we threw money around, lived to the hilt, bathed in champagne and had fleets of American cars, we were still quite responsible parents. All the children went away to a good school.'

But there were ups and downs with the youngsters. Her daughter Sue hated her mother turning up at school in a pink car and pink hairstyle.

Viv's present home lacks expensive furniture – but she is far happier curled up on her blue Habitat sofa watching TV than she ever was in the luxury bungalow.

'It is more cosy here,' she says. 'I would love to be able to replace the windows, but I can't afford it, so I don't worry. I have to really save hard if I want something. But then I don't crave things like I used to. I never wish I had more money because I know it only comes at a price.'

Vivian believes that Camelot must look after its winners. 'It may seem like a dream, but it can tear your life apart,' she says, adding that she and Keith received no professional advice on how to deal with their money.

'The Pools reps and solicitors gave Keith a lot of papers to sign and said we wouldn't have to worry about a thing, that everything would be taken care of. That was about it, really. With the lottery, they shouldn't let them win so young. I was twenty-three, look what happened. I dread to think how a sixteen-year-old would manage. I can't give them any advice. I just hope they cope better than I did.'

Viv may have regrets, but she is philosophical about the way she coped. 'I did as I said I would, and I would do the same again,' she says, 'Winning the Pools taught me how to spend and I had a lot of fun spending. But the money went. I've been skint for over twenty years. I kept trying to get a job but no one would have me. Everybody said, "You don't need the money." It was awful. I felt very hurt and frustrated. They all thought I had a load stashed away somewhere. Some still do!'

Instead Viv was living a poverty-line existence on her widow's pension.

Meanwhile Viv has a part-time job, which a friend offered her in 1993 at the Duty Free cosmetics and perfume shop in Wakefield's Ridings Centre complex. She works three days a week selling make-up to women. Two Saturdays a month she acts as a security officer.

'At least it allows me to buy a few extras to make myself look a bit better – and I get a discount on make-up,' she says. 'Maybe I'm helping the shop by pulling customers in as well. Even they can't believe I'm hard up. They must think the money lasts for ever.'

There was, of course, money from the book Viv co-authored and there was a television play, scripted by Jack Rosenthal, predictably called *Spend*. But Viv blew that too.

'I met Rosenthal just the once,' she reveals. 'He didn't want to see me any more as I think he had a preconceived idea of me. Actress Sue Littler played my part – she's dead now, but she became totally immersed in the role. It was a bit creepy. As I watched I thought – that's me – but I'd never do that in a million years. What was hilarious was the actors coming in and out of my house. I'd bump into someone who'd say to me, "Hello, I'm your dad, Joe Belcher." Then there was this actress playing my mother, puffing away at fags and knocking back the booze. My mother never drank or smoked in her life. It did make me cry at the end, though, when Gary, my third husband, died. The memory was still so vivid. He was on drugs but I only realised when it was too late.

'Looking back, I remember the day we did win and the draws kept coming in, Keith nearly cut his throat shaving. We wanted to celebrate and we had £1 between us. The copy of the Pools coupon was in an old pair of trousers which I'd just washed, but I rescued it and knew we'd won. So I borrowed a few quid from my dad, who hadn't cared much for Keith until then, extracted the family allowance from my mother, and off we all went to the local. I can still enjoy a drink, but not so much that I would end up behind bars. And I love clothes. I still have wardrobes full of them. They are my remaining extravagance. The jewels have all gone though.

'I once took part in a programme for Channel 4 on Pools winners and they sat me next to a man who'd won a million, I think. I asked him if he'd had any begging letters. He said yes but he'd junked them. I said, "Even the ones from me?" He couldn't see the funny side of it. Money buys you houses, cars, clothes and plane tickets but not laughter and joy. It has taken me thirty years to get back to normal and now that I'm poor but happy, I want to stay that way.'

And Viv would never even consider investing in a lottery ticket. 'I couldn't go through it all again. I honestly don't think I would survive it,' she says.

FOREVER CHAINED. Big spender Lee Ryan ties the knot with his live-in lover Karen Taylor a few weeks before appearing in court accused of stealing top-of-the-range cars. 'This is the best day of my life', he said. 'Winning £6 million is second best.'
(Courtesy Neville Chadwick)

FEEL GOOD FACTOR. Jobless Andy Voss and his family celebrate their win with champagne. Hours before scooping £3.9 million they couldn't afford a bottle of wine … and didn't even have a corkscrew. 'I'll swap my council house for a four-bedroom home that I can call my own,' he said. 'But I won't move to a swanky area.'
(Courtesy Express Newspapers)

HOWZAT! Cricket-loving Terry Benson won more than £20 million with the family he adored. But he still pledged to travel by bus every day. He told his nine-year-old grandson: 'As soon as I have cashed the cheque, there will be £2 million in the bank for you!' *(Courtesy Express Newspapers)*

WINNING MILLIONS WON'T CHANGE ME. Terry Benson hugs his wife Brenda to celebrate their £20 million jackpot. Hours later raiders burst their way into his house and helped themselves to his hard-earned bits and pieces. *(Courtesy Express Newspapers)*

YOU'RE A DOLL. Single mum Kathryn Brindle hugs her three-year-old daughter Leanne after winning £2,293,628 from her share of the jackpot prize. Leanne chose the winning numbers … then went back to her dolls. *(Courtesy Mercury Press)*

OUR PRIZE FAMILY. Bob and May Carruthers give one of their six granddaughters Abi a cuddle after celebrating their good fortune by buying them all Easter eggs. The £1 a week Lottery ticket was their only big gamble. *(Courtesy North News and Pictures)*

CELEBRATIONS WERE A WASHOUT FOR BOB AND MAY CARRUTHERS. They took a barge trip on the Norfolk Broads after scooping £2.4 million on the Lottery … but sailed into a week of storms. *(Courtesy North News and Pictures)*

HATS OFF TO SHAUN. The jobless air-conditioning fitter and his wife Jo, who have two children Shanna, aged two and four-year-old Calum, will never have to worry about paying the electricity bills again after winning £2.7 million in a day of good luck that began with the Grand National. *(Courtesy Express Newspapers)*

GOODBYE BIG SPENDER. Vivian Nicholson won £152,000 on the Football Pools in 1961 and vowed to spend, spend, spend. The win was worth around £2 million today. Now she hasn't got a bean but she is happier than she has been for years thanks to being a Jehovah's Witness. *(Courtesy Express Newspapers)*

Chapter Four

Life in the Fast Lane

> *'Dreams really can come true,*
> *We're in that land and how,*
> *And this weekend it could be you*
> *Fill out that ticket now.'*

These were the words of part-time poet and speed fanatic Lee Ryan as he celebrated scooping £6.5 million on the National Lottery, while on bail accused of stealing and handling top-of-the-range cars, among them a BMW and a Mercedes.

He soon proved to be a winner in the mould of Pools legend Vivian Nicholson. For he wasted no time splashing out with his share of the £13 million prize money from the March draw. The thirty-one-year-old, jobless, father of three and his partner Karen Taylor quickly moved from their £29,000 former council house in Branstone, Leicester, to a five-bedroom, £170,000, mock-Tudor, detached home near-by. But that was only a stop-gap. Bigger things were planned.

Out went the battered, Y-registration BMW and in came a £45,000 turquoise Jaguar XJR and a £130,000 Ferrari Testarossa. And that was only just the beginning of the spending spree. Well, why not?

'I bought the Jag because I had always promised myself one,' he told reporters hungry to find a lottery winner who would talk. They were as rare as the Great White Shark.

Lee and Karen, who had three children, planned to fork out another £1 million for a mansion built to order and equipped with a gym and swimming pool. They had bought their new detached, Tudor house as a transition home.

'We really want a place built with some land to it, where our children can roam free in a bit of space of their own,' said Lee, who was pleading not guilty to the charges against him when his case was heard by a jury at Crown Court.

'This house helps them make the change from the place where they were brought up to the bigger place in its own grounds. Having said that, I will miss the neighbours from the old place and I bought some of them presents.'

Although Lee was quick to abandon his humbler roots, his former neighbours said he had been generous with his new-found wealth. He ordered a black convertible BMW for Karen, whom he had lived with for fourteen years, offered to buy one of his best friends a new car and fly another to New Zealand.

'He's like a kid in a sweetshop with lots of money,' said a friend. 'He has always loved fast bikes and cars.'

Soon the Press would be following his motoring career with interest – and the Courts too.

One thing was for sure, Lee wasn't going to forget his parents either. A neighbour said, 'Lee has always wanted to look after his mum and dad, who don't live far away. He is giving them whatever they want. His home has always been immaculate and his kids have never wanted for anything. He is known around here as a great dad and a good family man. Now it will be like Christmas every day – and we say good luck to him.'

Because of his extravagance, Lee – who scooped his fortune for a £1 stake with the numbers 2, 13, 22, 27, 29 and 45 – seemed to have dashed any hopes of keeping his lottery win a secret. Camelot advisors were quickly on hand. 'Come clean,' they said.

On the chilly morning of Wednesday, 29 March, they unveiled him as a winner at the Café Royal in London. Determined not to let the prospect of a possible spell at Her Majesty's Pleasure tarnish his joy at winning, he faced the full glare of publicity at the hastily-called press conference. Hours before, Camelot had caused confusion by saying his partner, thirty-five-year-old Karen, had won the jackpot because her name was on the back of the ticket and she received the cheque. But Lee stressed to reporters that they were joint winners and they had chosen the numbers together.

'The decision to go public was entirely his own,' said Camelot. 'But his hand was probably forced when it became clear to people in his neighbourhood that he was spending a lot of money. He had been considering going public for some time and our advice to our big lottery winners is that if you intend spending a lot of money, it is very difficult to keep your win a secret.'

But the story did not end there.

Whilst Lee celebrated his jackpot, the Press was snapping at his heels. And finally his family revealed his secret sadness.

Car fanatic Lee was at the wheel of a Ford Cosworth sports car that spun out of control eight years before, hitting a lamp-post and killing his half-brother. The tragedy, in Heanor, Derbyshire, in 1987, had haunted his family ever since.

Lee was reluctant to discuss it at the press conference. He looked shocked when asked about his brother's death. Walking quickly away, he shouted, 'No comment, absolutely none!'

Back home in Braunstone, Leicester, office cleaner Ann Gumbs, fifty-nine, mother of Lee and his half-brother, was tearful.

'All this has brought back memories of my lost son,' she said. 'It is very painful. There is still a lot of hurt, but I'm happy Lee has won all this money. Everybody has got things in their past. I suppose that if you don't want people to know them, you shouldn't buy a lottery ticket.'

Her words were to echo the fears of families across Britain as they began to realise that when you go public, the public wants to know everything.

'As far as I am concerned, what is done is done,' Ann added. 'It's all public knowledge anyway. My husband is still very upset, he has been pacing the streets. There is still a lot of pain and hurt. Lee's win has brought it all back to him.'

A relative said, 'The family has never really got

over Paul's death. It is a living nightmare for Lee.'

Camelot was pressed by the Press too and defended its decision to pay out £6.5 million of lottery money to benefit Lee – a man with a criminal charge hanging over him. Camelot said it had no control over who bought the tickets.

Communications Director David Rigg stressed, 'Everyone in the country is fully entitled to play, and, if lucky, to win. We have no views on who receives the cash. It is our job to do what the law tells us, to make tickets available to everyone over sixteen regardless of the circumstances. With twenty-five million people playing every week, all sorts of people will be winners.'

The story deepened. For as if the glare of publicity hadn't blinded Lee enough by now, newspapers disclosed that he had been having five-times-a-week sex with a secret mistress and was with her on the night his family won the jackpot. As Karen was watching TV in her terraced home, Lee was allegedly with Melanie Thurman. Lee only realised his partner had won £6.5 million when he arrived home early the next day.

That afternoon the men and women from Camelot arrived. As they sat with him in his council house he told them that his win would not change his life . . . he didn't want to move. 'But he wanted to buy a £500,000 MacLaren F1,' said a lottery insider. 'When they asked him how he had felt the night before at eight o'clock after finding out he had won, he couldn't answer.'

Lee, thought of by many at Camelot as 'a really nice bloke', had never wanted publicity. But his secret love nest was exposed to the nation as a house near Huncote, Leicestershire, by the Press.

Melanie, twenty-six, told reporters how she thought Lee was unattached and never knew about his lottery jackpot. The affair ended the day he took her to collect a new £45,000 Jaguar saloon car after saying he had won lots of money.

On learning the truth, furious Melanie lashed out at Lee. 'He is a rat,' she said. 'He must be the last person on earth who deserves this good fortune. I cannot believe that he has done the dirty on me all this time.'

The world heard how Melanie had been living with another lover for eight years when she fell for keep-fit fanatic Lee. 'He had a great body and a hairy chest,' she said, and during their affair they tried more than 100 love-making positions. She believed he wanted to marry her. Dubbed the Poet Nauseate by the *News of the World*, Lee had written her a string of love poems which she had since burnt.

When confronted about his affair, Lee said, 'I won't contest anything Melanie says. It's over now and I just want to be left alone with my children to get on with my life. I'm no love cheat. A bloke will probably come forward next and say he had an affair with me.'

But Lee admitted Karen had given him a 'good quizzing' over the love-cheat claims in the newspapers.

Karen could probably have kept all of her £6.5 million jackpot, but she couldn't bear to walk out on Lee. And, even though she wrote her name on the ticket, making the fortune hers, she still insisted the millions belonged to both of them.

She revealed how Lee disappeared for days on end and couldn't control his violent temper. But when asked why she hadn't shown him the door she said, 'I love him because he is a rogue. He is always telling me how well we complement each other. Lee can be wild and a bit crazy but I bring him back down to earth.'

Her love had survived the humiliation of Lee's secret mistress telling the world how he regularly made passionate love to her – even on the night of his jackpot win.

'Lee told me she was just a friend and none of that was true, and I suppose I have to believe him,' said Karen. 'He's got lots of female friends because he's a very attractive man, but he's still here with me. The reality is that Lee probably hasn't been faithful to me all these years, though I've been faithful to him.

'Lee has never worked, he goes off for days on a friend's motorbike and I never know whether he's coming back or not. I've spent years going back and forward to the window, staring out and wishing he would come home. I have spent so long in that desperate state of not knowing where he is or who he is with, with my stomach churning. But I tell myself he is trying to find himself.'

The frustration was never greater than the night she was dying to tell her partner they had suddenly become multi-millionaires. Lee usually chose their lottery numbers, but that week Karen suggested selecting the figures linked to the children's birthdays.

Karen, who hadn't worked for thirteen years, surviving on £120-a-week state benefits, said, 'The kids and I were watching the lottery on TV and ticking off the numbers . . . they just kept coming up. We couldn't believe it. The kids were jumping around the room and going crazy. I was shaking with shock. I telephoned my mum and dad and they came round immediately. We tried to find Lee but no one knew where he was. It was impossible for me to take it all in and I was longing to tell Lee and share my feelings with him. He only came in around 2a.m. and by then Camelot had informed me of the amount, £6.5 million. They told me to put my name on the ticket.'

Karen and Lee lost no time throwing themselves into a hectic spending spree.

'I've bought lots of designer clothes for myself and the children,' she said. 'And I want to get my flabby body into shape with a personal trainer. I've always wanted to do horse riding, now I can get my own horse and Lee is going for helicopter lessons. Our philosophy is that we could drop dead tomorrow, so we want to enjoy the money now. I will probably get a cleaner, but I still want to wash the pots and try to keep life as normal as possible.'

There were gifts too – £25,000 each to several close friends, Karen's twin brothers and Lee's six brothers and sisters.

'Lee has always known he would be a millionaire one day and these things happening to him are no shock,' said Karen. 'But it is stressful; the other morning he threw a plate across the room and we had a terrible argument in the car showroom when he bought the new turquoise Jag, because I thought the colour was tacky.'

Karen's belief that money couldn't guarantee happiness was tragically borne out when her mum

Flo, sixty-five, died after suffering a critical heart condition. Speaking hours before her death in April, Karen said, 'I would give all the money back to make her better.'

Lee comforted Karen and blamed the pressure of publicity for helping to kill Flo. Devastated, he said, 'I'm not saying the pressure killed her directly, but it couldn't have helped. Money means nothing at a time like this. She was a very special lady.'

By now Lee was living in the fast lane. He had splashed out £500,000 from his winnings on a fabulous collection of high-performance cars and motorcycles. And his lottery luck was holding. For he survived two dramatic bike crashes in just three weeks.

First he smashed into a tyre wall at over 100m.p.h. while testing his flame-red Ducati 916 at Mallory Park race track, escaping with three bruised ribs. He just picked himself up, brushed himself down and jumped back on the £13,000 machine for a few more laps.

Weeks later he injured his wrist and shoulder when he collided with a Montego car at a set of traffic lights on his 160m.p.h. bike. The motorist escaped unhurt.

'I was dead lucky; there was a dent in the car roof where I head-butted it,' he said.

But there was no shortage of alternative transport while Lee's bike was out of action. He had bought another Ducati, an exclusive £17,000 SP version of the 916 capable of 170m.p.h. and he also had a £9,000 Kawasaki ZZR 1100 – at 178m.p.h. reputedly the fastest machine in Britain. But if he didn't fancy a bike ride there was always his new car fleet. Apart from the Jaguar and Ferrari he now had a Bentley Turbo R worth £132,000; a Porsche 911, a mere

£50,000; a Toyota Supra, £38,000; and a £30,000 Shogun.

High-flying Lee soon had a new craze however. He splashed out on a £250,000, five-seater helicopter. There was only one drawback – he couldn't fly. So he booked lessons. Meanwhile he hired a pilot at £400 an hour to take Karen on a shopping trip to London.

Although the couple had planned to build their own mansion, they soon fell in love with a beautiful farmhouse they had seen, complete with a lake, tennis court, swimming pool and forty acres of rolling green fields in West Leicestershire. While they were thinking about making an offer Karen picked up her new BMW – with a personalised numberplate of course.

There was only one thing missing in the couple's new life – marriage. And that wasn't such a big-spending affair as you might have expected.

The cars were by Ferrari and Bentley, the champagne by Marks and Spencer and the funding by the National Lottery.

'This is the best day of my life,' said Lee when he arrived for the ceremony at Leicester Register Office. 'The day I won £6.5 million was the second best.'

No exotic honeymoon was planned because Lee had to surrender his passport as part of his bail conditions while awaiting trial.

Karen, wearing a cream suit, drove to her wedding from their new home.

'It's a very low-key affair,' Karen said. 'We will have a fantastic time on a honeymoon somewhere in Britain, then after the court case we plan to go abroad and explore Peru.'

Lee told reporters, 'We haven't got a wedding list,

but if people want to present us with gifts then we won't say no.'

On August 4 the gleaming Bentley with the number plate Lee 4 glided to a halt outside Nottingham Crown Court as reporters, photographers and the public gathered on the pavement. Smiling, Lee lit a cigarette, left his lottery prize parked on double yellow lines as he entered the building on the seventh day of his secret trial. An hour later he wasn't smiling any more. For he was found guilty of taking a stolen BMW and Mercedes to Malta to sell. Both cars had false number plates and forged documents. The jury heard that Lee had a string of former convictions for burglary, assault and theft going back to the age of 14. Sentence was adjourned for reports. On his way to court that day he stopped to buy a scratchcard and won £2.

It was like any other Saturday night. The evening shadows glided around the doorsteps and the dancing colours of the TV screens flitted about behind the net curtains in the street that wound its way through the run-down area of Hartlepool, Cleveland, where unemployment topped twenty per cent.

Families sat in their front rooms, Dad with a can of beer, the kids on the floor and Mum walking in and out of the kitchen where chips and burgers were sizzling in their pans.

Outside the pavements glistened after the rain that day and little puddles had formed under the wheel-arches of the Ford Sierras and old Escort XR3s parked in the road.

Suddenly a piercing scream broke the silence. Front doors opened, curtains twitched and a man ran down the road to the telephone box shouting, 'We've won the lottery!'

It was a few minutes after 8p.m. on Saturday, 18 March, 1995, a date forever fixed in the memories of thirty-four-year-old jobless taxi driver Andy Voss and his wife Audrey, twenty-nine. For when the jackpot numbers 41, 19, 31, 18, 9 and 24 flashed up on the TV screen they realised they had won £3.9 million – and they couldn't stop screaming with joy in their terraced council house on the Oton Manor Estate.

Andy, who didn't have a telephone because he couldn't afford one, hot-footed it to the near-by kiosk with a handful of change, to invite friends and relatives for a drink to celebrate his good fortune.

'Audrey ran over and told us she had won nearly £4 million but she couldn't find a corkscrew,' said a neighbour. 'You could hear their shouts all over the street. We were delighted for them. The win couldn't have happened to nicer or more deserving people.'

The bottle-opener wasn't the only thing Andy and Audrey were short of after a year on State Family Benefits of £94.60 a week. Bottles of wine for the celebration bash had to be bought by relatives because they were completely broke.

'The £1 they put on the lottery was more or less the last few bob they had,' said Audrey's stunned mum Kathleen.

The party raged on until 2a.m., courtesy of Andy's brothers who provided all the dry white wine. The taxi driver who picked up some of the family from Andy's home in the early hours, said, 'The guy's dad came down the path skipping. He was over the moon, as they say. He wasn't drunk but he was very, very excited. He said his son had just won £4 million and was going to make sure his parents were OK. He was going to buy them a big, new bungalow and a car.'

The couple had been hoping to move to a three-bedroomed council house because their little boy and girl had to sleep in the same room. Now the world was their oyster.

Audrey bought the winning lottery ticket from her local newsagent's and general store on the Saturday morning. A woman behind the counter said, 'We don't really know her or Andy very well. They come in occasionally. But he turned up at seven the next morning, saying he'd won the jackpot and had been up all night.'

Jobless Fred Wallace, thirty-four, who was outside the shop at the time, told how Andy looked pale and seemed to be shaking. 'He couldn't believe he'd won and he had come to the shop to verify it. I've never seen a man so white,' he said.

Before giving up his job, Andy worked with taxi boss Dave Hudson for two years. Dave joked, 'I only hope he buys my company, times are really hard. This couldn't have happened to a nicer guy. His brother-in-law works for us and told us the good news.'

Andy had the last word. 'I'm going to swap my council house for a four-bedroom home that I can call my own,' he told reporters. 'But I won't be moving to a swanky area. I want to stay among the people I know best!'

The first thing he did though was to swap his eleven-year-old Vauxhall Cavalier for a new BMW.

For Camelot, the Vosses were ideal winners. By this time the lottery had created twenty-eight million-aires, but since controversy over Mukhtar Mohidin and his £17.8 million in December, most winners had opted for anonymity. Only twelve had signed Camelot's official form, renouncing their rights to privacy.

After weeks of bad press, a Commons inquiry into the naming of Mukhtar Mohidin, complaints about shortages of terminals and worries that the jackpot was too large, Andy's win seemed to be a turning point. Good publicity at last.

Winners of smaller jackpots, like single-parent Kathryn Brindle, also from Blackburn, who won £2.3 million on numbers picked by her three-year-old daughter Leanne, did not encounter the same pressures as the very big winners did. Leanne chose 4, 16, 25, 26, 31 and 43 and then went back to her dolls. The next day Kathryn was celebrating her instant elevation from Social Security recipient to double millionairess. She picked up her cheque for £2,293,628 from Sue Jenkins, who plays Jackie Corkhill in TV's *Brookside*. Her quarter share of the £9 million jackpot made her the third big winner from Blackburn. Was this Britain's luckiest town?

Kathryn's priority was to repay her daughter. She moved from her mother's terraced home to a house of her own.

'I always wanted a playroom for my little heroine, a bedroom of her own and a garden for her to play in,' said twenty-three-year-old Kathryn. 'It's the least I can do for her after this. Now she can have the life I always wanted to give her.'

Kathryn planned a holiday in the sun with little Leanne. She needed time to slow down and consider the future. But one thing was for sure.

'I am going to carry on living a normal life – although it will be a much more comfortable one,' she said.

Kathryn had forgotten the numbers her daughter had picked out when the lottery draw was shown on TV. 'I wasn't even watching,' she said. 'Then my sister came running in to tell me. I just didn't believe her at first.'

Kathryn had passed her driving test six months before, but had not been able to afford a car.

Like Mukhtar, she was an ardent fan of Blackburn Rovers, so she bought a season ticket. Now she watches her favourite team most weekends.

Ken Southwell, thirty-five, from Copmanthorpe near York, won £839,254, in the first lottery draw and believed he was honour-bound to share his reaction. He has still managed to keep his feet on the ground. In fact today he has become one of Camelot's best advertisements.

'You shouldn't be like a dog with a piece of meat and drag your good news into a corner so no one else can see it,' he said.

He believed Mukhtar would have saved himself a lot of anguish if he had been more open. 'It's going to come out in the end,' he said. 'Unless you have twenty-four-hour protection, plastic surgery and six months in the Bahamas, everyone will realise it's you eventually.' When he won, Ken had the Press camped out in the front garden. He soon became overwhelmed by the onslaught of investment advice and media attention. That was when Camelot's damage-limitation guru, Rick Dalgleish, rode to the rescue.

'Rick told me to come clean,' said Ken. 'He took me to a hotel for a couple of days to give me the space to absorb the impact. Now I can ring him whenever I want. Camelot's follow-through is brilliant.'

Engineer Ken quit work after his win and spent three months planning his investments. A sterling example of the popular 'I won't let it change my life' school of reaction, he was planning to find another job soon.

But winning has presented him with just one drawback. 'My ex-girlfriend came out with a story that was pure fabrication, saying I hadn't paid maintenance for my son. I could have sued them all to kingdom come, but I thought, "Let it pass." You can take a step back, don't waste energy getting aggressive.

'I'm high on being a millionaire, the stress is off, I can afford to be mature about these things. Winning this much has given me a small insight into how celebrities cope with being rich or famous.'

His careful modesty was much appreciated by the general public. They were nice to nice winners.

Ken's advice to anyone who wins is – don't panic. And don't make too many changes at once.

Since winning he has quit his job installing satellite dishes, moved into a five-bedroomed house with his girlfriend, bought a two-year-old Range Rover for £17,000, a new Suzuki jeep, a couple of other properties, which he rents out, and has put the rest into stocks and shares.

'I admit I don't have to worry about paying the next bill, but I still have to be careful,' he says.

His words rang true when he was seen bartering to get a discount on a new three-piece suite after offering cash. Why not, wouldn't we all?

'It took a long time getting used to having the money. It's only recently that I stopped waking up in the morning, thinking about it, though I'm still a little shocked by what has happened,' he says.

'I've spent all my life striving to get better qualifications, to get a better job in order to reach a position where I could earn more. Suddenly I had it all overnight. That takes some getting used to.'

Ken has become a sort of ambassador for Camelot, lapping up the pressure from the media hunters. He now offers advice on behalf of the National Lottery gurus to those who find it hard to cope.

'In those first few weeks I had a ball,' he says. 'At times it was quite scary, but everyone was good to me. It was funny being called a millionaire; you don't get called anything if you only have £50. Suddenly you realise what enormous power that sort of money brings.

'The amount I won was enough for me. If I'd been hit by £6 million like Lee Ryan or £10 or £12 million, that might have flipped my mind. The problem with that is your income is more than you can possibly spend, but I'm not against the big prizes. If people don't want that much money they can always give it away until they are down to what they can cope with. You quickly realise it's not about buying the Rolex watch, it's the little luxuries.

'I was doing a promotion with a magazine on top-of-the-range sports cars. Ferrari heard about it and sent a sales team to try to persuade me to splash out. They were disappointed that I didn't want to buy a car, but I'm a typical Yorkshireman – long pockets and short arms. I still give the Yorkshire war cry when I'm out shopping. You must have heard it. There are only two words: *How much?*'

Ken won £839,000. If he had scooped £17.8 million, would his words have been different, I wonder?

After seven months of enjoying semi-retirement, he was considering returning to work.

'I had been thinking about a change when the lottery win came up,' he said. 'Taking a few months off gave me a chance to look at my life. Financially I don't need to work again but my head wants to do something.

'I'm not the sort of person who sits at home and does nothing. I had a terraced house which I bought before the win and I've spent a lot of time doing that up. Just about every room in my new house has been redecorated.

'But there are only so many times you can polish the car and cut the lawn. After you've finished the chores, you wonder who to call? Then you realise all your friends are at work.

'I enjoy interacting with people and would like to do something in tourism; we'll see.'

The jackpot win has brought Ken fame in the area where he lives.

'People still walk into lamp posts in the street and say, "Are you him?"' he said. 'That doesn't bother me. I look on it as a nice form of envy. My friends have all been superb, they haven't reacted differently to me at all.'

His relationship with his girlfriend, whom he has been with for eighteen months, hasn't suffered either, despite the change of life style.

'If anything, it's ten times better,' he says. 'It's made me appreciate everything more.'

Occasionally he still does the lottery. 'If I'm meeting some friends in the pub on a Saturday night, I'll buy a couple of tickets and then at eight o'clock we check if we have won. I get ribbed about it, but it's friendly banter. Mind you, to win twice would be historic.'

He paused for a moment, 'One thing that does worry me, however, is that people can become obsessed about the lottery. I was in a shop the other day and saw someone buying £25 worth of tickets. I hope they don't do that every week.

'If it becomes an obsession, it's no longer fun. I hope we don't get to the stage where the National Lottery becomes a late twentieth-century disease.'

Ken does have one regret. His mother died a year before his win and he wishes she could have been around to enjoy his good fortune, as sons do.

'She always worried about me,' he says. 'It would have been wonderful if she was here now to share this with me.'

His neighbours in the village have been wonderful too. 'They come up and shake my hand like I've done something incredible,' he says. 'All I did was fill in a lottery ticket.'

Chapter Five

Winners and Losers

It was a warm but cloudy evening as Terry Benson strolled down to his near-by ex-serviceman's club for a £1.10 pint and a game of billiards, as he did every Saturday. When he arrived he saved a chair at his usual white, Formica table for his wife Brenda, who had worked for years as a factory packer. He laughed and joked with the bar staff and talked about cricket to his mates. At eight o'clock, sitting with his wife, he watched the *National Lottery Live* show on the club television set. Then, when the jackpot numbers started to flash up on the screen he went quiet. He thought he had at least five of them, but his ticket was at home. He tried to remember how he had chosen the numbers. He had walked around the foundry at work and picked the figures he saw dotted about on the machines. One of them was an identification code on a three-ton crane. Others were on metal castings and there were odd numbers scrawled on the walls. He wrote them down on a piece of cardboard in chalk and put it in his pocket.

From ten past eight to quarter past eleven when the hard-up maintenance electrician arrived back at his neat semi-detached house in Hull, he had hardly talked at all. He didn't want to say anything to his wife at the club because he didn't want to raise her hopes. As soon as they walked through the front door, Terry shot upstairs. He checked his ticket in the bedroom and shouted to Brenda, 'God, I think I have won! I think we've had some luck at last!'

The couple stared at the ticket.

'I don't think you have got the jackpot,' said fifty-six-year-old Brenda, 'because you haven't got the bonus number.'

The couple had won £20 million.

Camelot's prayers were answered. The Bensons were to be one of their happiest winning stories. There were no skeletons in the cupboard.

Two days later sixty-one-year-old Terry gaped at his giant cheque for £20,088,838 at a photo call and said, 'I don't want a new car – and I will still travel everywhere by bus.' Now he could buy 250 double-deckers.

It was a typical statement for the hard-working electrician who had been struggling to get by on £200 a week. The most important thing that he would be buying, he said, was security for his four children and six grandchildren for the rest of their days. He and Brenda were keeping half of the fortune. The other £10 million would be shared between his son and three daughters.

Then Terry turned to his nine-year-old grandson

Stephen and said, 'As soon as I have cashed the cheque, there will be £2 million in the bank for you.'

Terry, who got up at 5.30a.m. each morning to catch the bus to work at Starkeys foundry near his home, filled in his lottery ticket of twelve lines with £2 each from members of his family. It was only the second time that they had entered together.

They decided from the start not to keep their win secret because they did not want to lie to their friends. In the roll-over draw they were the only people in Britain to pick all six numbers 1, 3, 11, 14, 20 and 40.

The family all raced to Terry's home when they heard the news. Then they stayed up all night toasting their win on the tiny patio until the small hours.

'We kept hearing whispers and the tinkling of glasses,' said a neighbour.

The next day, Brenda owned up. She told a friend, 'We're going to London. It looks like we have won thousands.'

Hours later a fleet of Mercedes cars rolled up to collect the family.

There was more good news for Camelot when Terry's daughter-in-law, Sue, told reporters, 'We have always been the happiest family in the world. After all the horrible things I have read about lottery winners, it is nice that this fantastic win should go to people like us. I married into this family fourteen years ago and they really are the loveliest people I know.'

But others weren't so pleased for the Bensons. Once more the gods of greed and envy reared their ugly heads.

A few days later Terry and Brenda came back to earth with a bump. They found their home had been burgled while they were away celebrating their £20 million win. But cricket-loving Terry, who lost jewellery of great sentimental value in the sneak raid, took the setback in his stride. He said outside his £35,000 semi, 'We'll not let the low life responsible for this get us down. We'll get over it, just as we have had to get over other blows over the years. I am devastated. No one likes intruders prowling about their home. I wonder what they would feel like if it happened to them.' He offered a substantial reward for the return of the pearl necklace he bought Brenda for their thirtieth wedding anniversary seven years earlier. He also hoped the thieves would return a gold watch-strap turned into an identity bracelet, which had belonged to Brenda's dead mother, Molly.

The early morning raid by two men raised questions about the security provided by Camelot. Friends criticised the promoters for whisking the Bensons, their son and three daughters away to a cheque presentation in the south leaving only a seventy-one-year-old woman neighbour in charge of the house.

Camelot quickly reviewed security for future winners, considering the possibility of providing professional guards while homes were left empty. The thieves had torn off a back patio door and ransacked the house.

A police spokesman said, 'It is obvious that the Benson home was singled out because of all the publicity.'

The intruders were seen near Terry and Brenda's home at about 2a.m. One resident said, 'There were crowds of Press and TV people calling at the house throughout the day. Everyone thought the people in the Bensons' garden were just more pressmen. Some were still knocking at the door around midnight.'

Terry's plea for the return of the sentimental items worked however. The pearl necklace and the gold bracelet were found following an anonymous telephone call. Terry was philosophical, feeling the raid was all part of life's rich and rocky pattern. It was destiny.

One man who definitely felt the call of destiny was Scottish Highlands publican Bill Petrie. He was so convinced that he had to buy a lottery ticket that he travelled 116 miles to get one.

Father-of-two Bill, of the Tipsy Laird pub, in Kingussie High Street, had to buy his single ticket each week in Inverness. Then in November 1994, after filling in and paying for his usual card, he bought another when he returned home and discovered that a lottery machine had finally been fitted at his local newsagent's.

The next evening his away-day ticket netted him a cool £155,500 – and his local bet scooped him a tenner!

'I got a bit tipsy on Saturday night when I realised I had won,' said Bill. 'Everyone in the bar got a free drink. The whole town was buzzing with the news of the big win and the pub was packed to the door. It was a night I will never forget.'

Bill was one of seventeen winners in Britain who scooped £154,828 with five correct numbers that weekend. If he had picked 20 as his other number, he would have become a multi-millionaire.

But winning millions would not make everyone happy.

Lottery runner-up Bill Reid, who picked up £330,000 said, 'Thank God I didn't win the jackpot.'

He claimed he would rather have jumped off a cliff than win £17.8 million like Mukhtar. He would have handed back the cash rather than be faced with the pressure a win of that size would bring, he claimed.

'I feel sorry for any family that wins the jackpot because their lives will be made a misery,' he said. 'They will be hounded to the ends of the earth and never be left in peace. I am so glad that it did not happen to me.'

The sixty-four-year-old labourer and great-grandfather was sitting comfortably in the lounge of his home when the winning lottery numbers flashed up on the TV screen as he watched one of his favourite programmes, Cilla Black's *Blind Date*.

Suddenly he leapt from the chair with delight because he thought he had won £10 after his three regular numbers came up.

'I nearly hit the roof,' he said. 'I was jumping up and down and going crazy. I was a bit gob-smacked when I realised I had won more than £300,000.'

Then came a comedy of errors, because Bill and his fifty-nine-year-old wife Shirley could not find the ticket. They spent an hour searching for it, finally discovering it in a shopping bag.

'But when we finally found it, we couldn't read the numbers properly because we've both got bad eyesight,' he said.

Within weeks they had planned a holiday to New Zealand and gifts for their three children, eleven grandchildren and four great-grandchildren.

Bill's views were shared by another £330,000 winner, Helen Sutton.

'I don't know what I would have done with £17.8 million,' she said. 'I would have been happy winning £10. I'm delighted to have won of course, but I don't envy families who hit the jackpot. I would like to shake their hands and wish them luck because their win is going to change their lives for ever.'

Helen, twenty-one, from Bridgend, Mid Glamorgan, who was earning £4.50 an hour as a crime records clerk at South Wales Police HQ, and dating a young bobby, had already picked up £10 the previous week. She won her little fortune after re-investing £5.

She chose her winning numbers by writing 1 to 49 on scraps of paper, turning them over and then picking them out with a pencil. She was at work on the 10p.m. to 6a.m. shift that Saturday when her mother rang to tell her she had won £337,644. When her boss heard how much she had got he asked if the local force could have a loan.

'They were that hard up,' said Helen.

She declined the request, went out and bought herself a £200 leather jacket and a big Mac with fries at McDonald's.

It was a cool April morning as the car made its way down the winding village high street and stopped outside the newsagent's shop.

The driver had a smile on his face as he went in to buy a newspaper and some sweets . . . and he was smiling when he came out. In fact the locals had noticed that Arthur Perry had been smiling a lot over the last few weeks. But inside he didn't feel as cool as the crisp, April air. The sixty-one-year-old coach-firm boss could hardly go on much longer with the stress of his burning secret. Finally he cracked and rang a local newspaper reporter.

'I'm a lottery millionaire,' he said.

Making the confession was a weight off his mind – now he could get on with his life. For Arthur was one of fourteen lucky winners to share April's £18.9 million National Lottery jackpot.

When his numbers came up he quickly told Camelot, 'Don't tell anyone – I don't want any publicity.'

But the strain of not telling anyone except his sixty-year-old wife, Irene, became too much. After he got his local newspaper to put the story on page one, he said, 'I should have gone public from the word go! Keeping quiet and containing my pleasure was the most difficult thing I have ever done. I'm so relieved that everyone knows. At first we wanted to keep our feet on the ground and get used to having the money. But somehow the secret began leaking out and it was more difficult avoiding the gossip than coming clean. It's the best thing we have done since winning. The villagers have been marvellous. They are as pleased as we are.'

Arthur and Irene, of Weaverham, near Northwich, Cheshire, bought two new cars and shared their £1.3 million fortune with their two children and three grandchildren.

And what was the former Navy radio operator's foolproof system of picking the winning line? He juggled his old Service number.

Things do sometimes go right when you win the lottery. Take smiling chimney sweep David Cook, from Norwich. He ordered a new MG sports car when he won. Reg Duff, a painter and decorator from Purfleet, Essex, who won £987,000, went out and bought a new Mercedes saloon, then booked a cruise to New Zealand. Anne Morgan from Devon, finally had enough money for flying lessons; Norman Flair from Melton Mowbray, fifty-four, proposed to his long-term girlfriend on Valentine's Day because he could finally afford to pay for the wedding; stewardess Wendy Norris, who picked up £338,715, bought the Corvette she had always wanted; and Angela Shaw finally had enough money to pay for treatment to stimulate the eyesight of her son who suffered from cerebral palsy. Such people were Camelot's best advertisement.

One man, however, who did not end up a good advertisement for winning a fortune was Barry Dunstan, now forty-nine. He was the first ever £1 million winner of Express Newspapers' Millionaires' Club competition in 1984 and when it came to spending he was in the Vivian Nicholson class. He had thirty-eight classic cars, an indoor pool and blew £15,000 in an hour at Harrods.

Today he is bankrupt and has returned to live with his mother in the Cornish town of Chacewater, where he was born. He is £20,000 in debt, doesn't even have a bank account and works as a £100-a-week tyre fitter. But even though he's skint, Barry says he doesn't regret a moment of those crazy, wonderful, hellish years.

'If I won another million I would do it all again,' he vows. 'It's the kind of person I am and I can't change that. But I have learned some hard lessons. I've found that money corrupts – not the people who've got it, but the people around the people who've got it. When you are a millionaire you find you have suddenly got loads of friends. And you can't blame people who are skint for trying to get money out of a millionaire. I would have tried it myself. But you learn about people. About the terrible, awful things they will do for money. It's sad.'

It is hard to believe that just a few years ago, the man who is back living with his eighty-one-year-old mother, was the owner of a 120-acre estate in Wales, four blocks of flats and investments worth £300,000. His ten-bedroomed mansion, Glandwr Hall, had gold-plated radiators in the rooms and every bedroom had a bathroom complete with gold fittings. He also installed a £100,000 indoor swimming pool covered by a Victorian glass conservatory and set up a classic car garage in the estate's outbuildings. 'I spent £250,000 doing up that place,' Barry told the *Daily Express*.

So what happened? Where did it all go? Lottery punters need to know.

'I won a million and I spent it,' Barry shrugs. 'It was as simple as that really. People keep telling me I should have been more sensible and invested more. But I couldn't see the point. It wasn't making anyone happy. It wasn't giving people jobs – apart from those good-for-nothing leeches, the accountants. So I uninvested it and spent it. Viv Nicholson's motto might have been spend, spend, spend, but she had absolutely nothing on me!'

No kidding. Barry was a £120-a-week carpet-cleaner salesman before his win. The day he scooped the million pounds he blew £15,000 in Harrods.

'I bought a £9,000 Swiss watch and matching Dupont lighter, a gold Rolex for £3,500, sixty pairs of shoes, a suit and 100 pairs of underpants, all in one hour,' he says. 'It was a terrific feeling. There I was in scruffy jeans and a T-shirt splashing out. I'd had to get a £100 bank loan to get me and my mum Betty to London for the presentation hosted by Jeremy Beadle.'

From there he went on holiday to Jamaica. 'I met singer Johnny Cash on the island and we both gave £10,000 to a home for local orphans,' he says.

In Montego Bay he met and fell in love with a black waitress called Princess and paid £1,000 for her to have electricity installed in her house.

'I was all set to marry her,' says Barry. 'I came within an inch of chucking Britain for good.'

Barry had already been married twice. Wife number one was Welsh-born Mai, whom he married in 1967. They had three children, but divorced in 1972. Wife number two was Irish redhead Patricia, now forty-seven. They married in 1978 and separated two years later.

But Princess did not become wife number three.

'I flew home and went to Wales to be reunited with the kids. I hadn't seen them for nine years,' he says. 'Then I fell for the barmaid in the local pub.'

Her name was Jeanne Fairlamb and a few months later they married in a romantic ceremony on Valentine's Day in 1986.

'Jeanne and I had a honeymoon which set me back

£20,000. There was a Concorde flight to Miami and a sixteen-day cruise,' he says. 'But the marriage lasted just two years. She left me because of my drinking.'

At the time of the split, Jeanne said, 'Barry's problem was that he would listen to everybody else's advice. He was hopeless with money and sometimes I couldn't bear to watch. Everyone tried to stop him throwing it all away but he did whatever he wanted. He once told me, "It's my money and I can do what I want with it!" He has done and now it is all over.'

To console himself, Barry went on more spending sprees. He thought nothing of paying £100 for a round of drinks.

'I even wrote a cheque for £50,000 once because a bloke needed to sell two houses,' he says. 'I bought them to make him happy.'

He also had holidays in Trinidad, Tobago, Mexico and the Maldives and bought a new Jaguar XJS and ten Triumph Stags.

'It was easy to spend. I thought it would just last for ever and ever.'

But every money-making scheme Barry tried failed. Every investment crashed.

'I lost £250,000 in the 1987 Stock Market Crash,' he says. 'So I drew out what I had left and spent it. It was a mistake. If I'd left it where it was, it would have earned me £1.6 million a year later.'

Not long after the split with Jeanne, Barry met freelance writer Sharon Appleyard, a divorcee with three children, and swept her off her feet with his cavalier charm. One night, true to style, he blew £40 on a taxi fare just to find flowers to take to her home in Truro, Cornwall. They married and lived in luxury at his manor house for two and a half years. Sharon ditched him three years ago, saying, 'I wanted for nothing, he granted my every wish. If I just mentioned something he would buy it. He even built horse stables when I wanted to take up riding. His wealth seemed like a bottomless pit but it became suffocating. He was protective and it got to the stage where if I had to go to the shop he would have built a supermarket in the grounds of the house to save me the trip. All the time he was drinking. He was too drunk for me and I was too selfish for him.'

Barry says sadly, 'I still love Sharon, still dream about her. But I know that these women would not have looked at me twice if I hadn't had money. To me, winning a million was THE BIG DREAM. When I was a kid, Mum and I used to sit in front of the TV before the football results and we'd plan how we'd spend our Pools win. My dream was to build a bungalow with a workshop and a filling station behind it. I'd play with cars all day, take holidays and just relax. But when the dream came true, I didn't do it. I was too busy spending.'

Barry is writing a book about the past ten years, to be called, of course, *Who Wants to be a Millionaire*?

'I'm doing it to tell people not to wish their lives away dreaming about money. A million quid doesn't make everything OK. I've lost the two women I really loved, I had to check into a drying-out clinic because I was drinking myself to death, my friends have disappeared and now I'm alone. But I hold on to one big dream – to find a woman who loves me for myself.'

Barry still drinks a lot. And the more he drinks, the sadder he seems. No matter how often he insists that he's happier now, his words ring hollow.

'I really do enjoy tyre fitting,' he says. 'It gives me enough money to get by, keeps me physically fit and I'm among friends. I've spent three years selling the watches, the paintings and the furniture to pay the bills. But the cupboard is bare now. Sometimes when I buy a £3 bottle of plonk, I recall the days when I stocked my cellar with vintages at £200 a bottle. But remembering doesn't hurt me. I'm a better person now! If I'd worked to earn a million, then lost it, I'd be gutted. But because I won it, it's different. Everyone thinks it's a magical figure and when you get it, you'll never have to work or worry again. But who knows how long it will last? I thought it would last for ever and I was wrong. How the hell does someone like me know what a million quid is? When you win a million, you don't need a financial adviser. You need a psychiatric adviser.'

Perhaps Barry could have done with the advice of TV's favourite agony aunt, Denise Robertson, who appears regularly on ITV's *Good Morning* programme with Richard and Judy. She says, 'Funnily enough, Viv Nicholson and I participated in a phone-in the other day, giving advice to lottery winners.

'We got the story of one couple who had won quite a trivial amount and had immediately been bombarded with suggestions about what to do with the money from friends and family who, apparently, got quite offended if the couple did not rush to take their advice.

'What I would say to anybody who wins is do absolutely nothing. Remain anonymous, go to ground until you have settled down – and then do what you want to do. What you need is space, time to think.

People do not think it through. The unfortunate thing is that you are impaled on a tidal wave of euphoria and what you do impulsively can turn out to be destructive.

'I don't think money in itself is destructive. Certainly £1 million is not enough to revolutionise your life for ever. But then, like Barry Dunstan, all of a sudden you find yourself with the battle scars. He had it, he blew it, and now he must write it down to experience. After all, he has had a fantastic experience and has gained great knowledge. He has been on a round the world trip. He has seen things he wouldn't have seen, experienced emotions he would never have known. He should now look around, make the best of what he has got and get on with the rest of his life. The £1 million isn't a tombstone, it's a blessing which misfired. But I do feel sorry for him. I think the organisations responsible for dishing out large sums of money like Camelot should say, "You have won this fortune, but you cannot have it for eight weeks!" It would give a winner breathing space, time to think.'

But many of Britain's lottery winners were not giving themselves time to think. They were screaming with delight on a Saturday evening and banking their millions on the Monday.

One man shouting with delight was a forgetful father of six, Ron Marron. He emerged as the missing millionaire in a June draw after his winning lottery ticket fell out of a book where he had put it for safe keeping.

Camelot knew there were seven winners in the £10.3 million jackpot draw and sixty-year-old Ron was the only one in Britain not to have claimed his share.

Ron, from Tyldesley, Greater Manchester, General Secretary of the Association of Metal Workers, who spent up to £40 a week doing the lottery, forgot about the ticket after tucking it away in the book he used as treasurer of a pub darts league. He only found it by chance when it fluttered to the floor as he was leafing through the pages on the following Wednesday.

His daughter Tracy emptied their dustbin to find a discarded Sunday newspaper with the draw numbers on. When they checked the ticket Ron discovered he was £1,481,262 better off.

A clairvoyant had given another daughter, Susan, a lucky stone which she had rubbed a few minutes before the big draw.

But even if your luck is in and you win the jackpot, it doesn't mean that the luck will stay with you forever, as Bob and May Carruthers discovered.

They were blissfully ignorant of their £2.4 million win for four hours in April. They were more interested in catching their granddaughter's stage debut at a local theatre in Silksworth, Tyne and Wear, than in checking their Camelot card.

'It was midnight when I got back and checked the numbers,' said Bob, sixty-seven. 'When we discovered we had won we couldn't sleep and ended up ringing the whole family.'

The doting couple with three daughters and six granddaughters, went out and celebrated by buying them all Easter eggs.

'We do not drink and apart from spending a pound a week on the lottery we never gamble,' said retired insurance agent May, also sixty-seven.

Two months later they pushed the boat out – with a barge trip on the Norfolk Broads. But it turned out to be a wash-out as storms swept the area. The couple, awash with cash and shivering, were awash with depression as they finally abandoned their rain-lashed boat for the comforts of bed and breakfast.

The trip had gone from bad to worse, as they were unable to find moorings every night.

'It was atrocious,' said Bob.

No-frills Bob had won our hearts when he said the cash wouldn't change him, come hell or high water. Having experienced both, the couple were planning to fly to Australia and had booked a cruise to New York on the QE2, returning on Concorde, of course.

Some people seem destined never to win a lottery anywhere in the world, regardless of whether their numbers come up or not. The joy of winning for some is eclipsed by the pain of losing for others.

Take the housewife in Huddersfield who gave the National Lottery numbers to her husband to enter on his way to work. She was celebrating their multi-million pound win with the neighbours when he returned home to reveal that he had forgotten to stop off at the newsagent's with her entry. The champagne suddenly went flat and so did their marriage for a day.

Another mother faced a bleak Christmas after losing a National Lottery ticket worth £46,800. Yvonne Whitehead, forty-nine, who lived on income support, left the ticket on top of the freezer. But the next day, when she realised she had a winning combination, the ticket had disappeared.

'It was a nightmare – it would have made such a difference to our lives,' said Yvonne who had two children aged twelve and eleven. 'It must have blown away. In the end we just accepted it was lost and we wouldn't ever see the money.'

The family stripped their home in Brampton, near Rotherham, three times in their frantic and futile search.

For some who manage to hold on to their winning tickets things are never what they seem. For over an hour on 14 January, some lucky punters thought they had scooped a £19.4 million jackpot in the National Lottery. But there were 133 winners with all six numbers correct. Sadly, this was among the factors slashing the first prize money to just £122,510 each.

There are those however, who, no matter how hard they try, simply do not have the knack of winning anything at all. Like hard-up Kenny Clarke who blew a £4,800 windfall. Kenny, forty, was left the nest-egg by a friend in his will. He knew he should invest the cash but he didn't fancy stocks and shares and so he staked £400-a-week for twelve weeks on the National Lottery, but never won a penny. By then he couldn't even afford the wallpaper he needed to do up his two-bedroomed bungàlow, so he plastered the walls with the spent tickets.

Kenny, of Clacton, Essex, bought a black cat called Lucky and changed the name of his home to 'The Lottery', hoping it would bring him a win. 'No chance,' he said, 'and the cat ran away after two saucers of milk. I haven't seen it since. I did every permutation I could think of. Then I did a set of numbers picked out of a hat. When my money ran out I thought about doing the Pools . . . they seemed to be better value. But I decided to continue with the decorating by using the lottery tickets as a reminder of how daft I had been. I'm still doing the lottery of course, but my motto now is that you can win with one line just as easily as you can with 100. I just hope someone else remembers me in their will, though.'

A Camelot spokesman said, 'It must be the most expensive wallpaper ever. But he shouldn't stop trying to win.'

There is a moral somewhere in the story of Kevin Hatcher and Paul Titchmarsh. Luckless Kevin, eighteen, pulled out of his two-man syndicate to let his friend take over because he couldn't afford the 50p stake. A few weeks later Paul, twenty-seven, from Hothfield, near Ashford, hit the jackpot with £877,000. Painter and decorator Paul, who is married to Tina, thirty-three, and had not been able to work for three years since an accident in which his best friend was killed, said, 'Kevin told me he couldn't afford to gamble any more. After we won, he came round to congratulate me. I might give him a fiver to cheer him up, but nothing more.'

Jobless Kevin was sporting about it. 'I'm starting to feel pretty sick about the whole thing, but I didn't pay the money, so I didn't win,' he said. 'It would have been great to have all that cash, but I'll get over it. I am still young and there's plenty of time to make my fortune.'

Paul planned to adopt his three stepchildren, take them to Disneyworld and replace his old Ford Sierra with a Porsche.

Tina said, 'We've had our troubles, now we hope to put them all behind us.' Her niece was killed in a road accident in which Paul's uncle had also died. But good luck was now running in the family. Paul's mother Alberta, fifty-two, won £300,000 with her husband Michael.

Alberta, from Challock, had to give up her job as a school caretaker after a heart attack. Now she was buying a bungalow. 'We're so pleased Paul and Tina won,' she said. 'They have had nothing but problems because of Paul's ill-health. Everybody out there deserves a win as long as it doesn't change what they are.'

Chapter Six

Lucky Numbers

Gambling on the lottery is not like gambling on a horse. There is no real form to go on. But you can bring the odds on winning down from that frightening fourteen million to one. Some people have an odd way of trying to do this – but sometimes it works. They seem to stumble on success with methods such as copying the numbers from their electricity meters, leading the dog to a plate of numbered biscuits or using the price coding on packets of cornflakes.

Superstition, it seems, cannot be disentangled from our enjoyment of the game.

Even Camelot realises this, because they run a TV advert with an elderly man visualising his winning combination in the pattern of a pile of bricks. Mystic Meg meanwhile, ever ready to offer us her predictions, even if they do take some believing, is another symptom of our desire to know the unknowable.

The tried and tested method of using birth dates and telephone numbers might just come up with the winning line for the lottery – although experts say this reduces the changes of a giant payout because so many people use it. Alternatively you could try to clean up by using the increasingly popular, if rather bizarre, device of putting ping pong balls inside a tumble dryer and picking them out after a quick spin. So far, though, this seems to have been something of a wash-out, with no big winners reported.

Melanie Thomas scoffed at her boyfriend Andrew Green's method of entering the lottery. He cut up a cereal box and wrote all the numbers on the bits of cardboard, then he put them in a giant Smarties tube, shook them up and the first six to come out were the ones he entered on his ticket.

But Melanie, twenty-three, from Portsmouth, Hampshire, isn't complaining any more. For twenty-two-year-old Andrew won £98,000 when five of the numbers came up.

In January 1995, TV's cleverest maths mistress, Carol Vorderman, was telling us that the odds against winning the UK jackpot were 13,983,816 to 1 but that, after just eight draws, a pattern was beginning to emerge that might enable us to reduce those odds. Number 44, for example, was red hot. It had been drawn four times. Both 3 and 5 had dropped out of the 'tumble dryer' three times and so had 30 if you included the bonus numbers. By working out the 'hot' and 'cold' numbers, which would become more obvious the longer the lottery ran, you could choose the numbers which the law of averages says must be due to fall. Cold numbers are the ones which haven't 'performed' for some time.

Of course, the spinning balls come out of the machine totally at random, with no possible pattern or predictability. But some numbers do have an intriguing habit of emerging more often than others. By 8 April, for example, the numbers 17, 29, 31 and 42 had popped out an impressive six times since the megadraw started in November. But 1, 8, 33, 34, 39, 40 and 45 had been chosen only once.

The best way to keep track of the hot and cold numbers is to make your own simple chart. Write the numbers 1-49 down the left-hand side of a page and the dates of the draw, past and future across the top. Each time a numbers appears mark it with an X. You'll soon see which ones hit regularly and which ones are missing. Then it's up to you to use your own judgement to decide when a hot number has come to the end of its run.

There are other ways of looking at past draws to help you decide what to pick and what to avoid. For instance, on 10 December the draw hit only high numbers. The following week the draw produced mostly lows. Only one was above fourteen and the total came to eighty-two. If you like to play the highs and lows, work out from your table the hottest numbers under twenty-five and the hottest ones above.

It's the same for odds and evens. You could try playing only the hottest odds for example. Or just the hottest evens. In this way, maybe you can make the law of averages work for you after all.

A mathematician once came out with an amazing theory of probability. He reckoned that if you sat a monkey down long enough with a typewriter, eventually it would produce the entire works of Shakespeare

– without a single spelling mistake. There is a snag in putting this theory to the test. You would have to wait longer than the lifetime of the universe for the monkey to complete its task. On the other hand there are those of us who do not have to wait for the law of averages to lend a hand. Some of us are simply born lucky.

In February 1995 a National Lottery worker had won a prize in the contest every week since it started. Commissionaire Carmel Bellizzi, forty-eight, worked at Camelot's area office in Shirley, West Midlands. He forked out £10 a week with his random numbers and his gambling fever had come up trumps, netting him £500 in the twelve draws. Each week he persuaded his five children to help complete the coupons. His biggest win was £160 – but Carmel of Hollyrood, Birmingham, is still determined to net the jackpot. 'I'm still waiting for the big win,' he says.

Let's not forget Arthur Kimbarley, the seventy-year-old former butcher from Headington, Oxford, who cashed in on every draw for the first fifteen weeks of the lottery. He spent £5 a week, and still does; his winnings so far total £2,000.

In the USA, in March 1994 offers were flowing in for a battered van because both its owners had become millionaire lottery winners. When Betty and John Taylor bought the 1991 pick-up in 1993, they knew its previous driver had put it up for sale after scooping £3 million. Then the Taylors landed their own £5.2 million jackpot in the Florida Lotto contest. And although hundreds of other players were telephoning their Port Orange home daily trying to buy the lucky brown truck, Betty, fifty-two, says, 'It's not for sale at any price. Who knows? It could bless us again.'

Trying to give fate a helping hand is hardly fool-proof, as millions of us know. But housewife Sally Barnes reckons she may be the brains behind a Staffordshire postman's £1.8 million jackpot win.

She devised her own numbers formula and gave about sixty copies of her booklet *Win the Lottery* to friends. Thirty-five of them won. But her biggest thrill came when the postman hit the jackpot just three weeks after she claims she gave him the brochure. Sally herself has only won £100.

Meanwhile one lucky couple got the shock of their lives after winning £800,000 in the lottery – with numbers chosen from their electricity bill. Bright sparks Joseph and Dawn Airey had been using their account number and meter readings since the lottery began. Their idea had already netted them three £10 wins before a £796,183 windfall came along. Joseph, forty-two, of Prestwich, Greater Manchester, immediately quit his job as a forklift truck engineer. He originally chose numbers from the Norweb bill because it was lying around and Dawn, thirty-eight, was in a rush to go shopping.

'If it hadn't been for Dawn being in such a hurry we might never have won,' he said.

The couple picked five numbers plus the bonus ball. 'I felt numb when they told us how much we'd won,' said Joseph. They bought a new car, went looking for a new house and planned an exotic holiday. But the first job was to pay for driving lessons for daughter Emma, seventeen. Their nineteen-year-old son, computer operator Geoff, meanwhile had his eye on something racy with four wheels.

'We certainly don't have any problems paying our electricity bills now,' said Dawn.

Another lucky lottery couple, Peter and Eunice MacLeod, bought two tickets instead of one by mistake . . . and doubled their winnings. But when Peter arrived home with a ticket for his wife, he found she had already bought one – with the same numbers.

Peter, fifty-one, a council roadman, demanded his £1 back from Eunice, forty-four, a supervisor at Raigmore Hospital, Inverness. But his annoyance turned to delight when five of their six numbers came up, winning them £1,850 each.

'I feared I had wasted the extra £1, but Lady Luck must have been smiling on us both,' he said.

A study of the lottery jackpot winners shows that the finger of fortune points mostly at male manual workers who buy five or fewer tickets a week. Men named John have won more major prizes than anyone else, followed by Davids and Williams. Men appear to be luckiest, despite equal numbers of males and females playing. Six months into the draw, men had claimed sixty-two per cent of the jackpots. The analysis was based on the profiles of 120 people who had won more than £50,000 each. Most said they chose their numbers at random using a combination of methods – from dartboards to bingo machines. Only two in ten used birthdays and other special dates.

The Scots are the keenest players although they do not win more often than people in any other region of the country. Most winners come from the biggest cities, despite claims by Blackburn and Sunderland to be the luckiest towns in the country. And interestingly, nearly all the near-millionaires won a small prize before snapping up a fortune.

The luckiest job is that of a manual worker, a profession which has taken more than half of the top prizes, with those in construction getting the lion's share. Housewives account for just three per cent of wins so far.

The identikit picture of a hard-core, heavy lottery spender was already emerging over the first six months of the game. According to the Henley Centre, he or she was likely to be a Scot, aged between twenty-five and thirty-four, who earned between £9,500 and £15,000 a year, liked gambling on the horses, reading a tabloid newspaper and sitting slumped in front of the TV for more than twenty-nine hours a week.

So it would seem that one method of standing a better chance of winning would be to change your name to John, become a builder, be aged in your thirties, be a couch potato and move to London, Manchester or Glasgow.

If that doesn't work, boffins at VCI Software have helpfully devised a computer programme to assist you pick numbers. But buyers should note the commendably honest small print on the back of the pack. 'The publishers do not claim that any numbers are more likely to win than others,' it says.

The software costs £14.99. But pins cost 10p a packet and are probably just as effective in selecting those all-important figures.

National Lottery, The Winning Guide, is a video

containing more than twenty tips and strategies presented by Channel Four racing expert John McCririck. In it he tackles hot and cold numbers, probability, aggregate totals and the art of wheeling.

The video tells us to avoid birthdays and anniversaries because these restrict you to only sixty-three per cent of the available numbers and you are battling against everyone else.

Avoid lucky numbers. These all tend to be prime numbers – 3 and 7 are favourites. Again you are likely to be using the same numbers as many other people.

We humans are notoriously bad at being random. We are afraid of using numbers which are clumped together because they don't look random. So don't space your numbers out just because you think they don't look random enough. Try to outsmart everyone else. Pull your numbers out of a hat if necessary. Anything as long as it is random.

Remember the frightening fact that there are fourteen million combinations. So spot trends and keep a record of the numbers drawn each week, says John. Ignore astrological predictions in newspapers. They put you into the same thought processes as millions of other people. Buy your ticket in time. Don't leave it to the last minute. It doesn't matter what day or time you enter, but avoid the last-minute rush. And keep your ticket safe, he advises. Try to have a routine. Store it in the same place each week.

His most interesting tip puts us into the magical world of wheeling. For a £7 entry of seven lines you will need a pool of seven numbers. With this combination, he says, if you win the jackpot you will also get second prizes. But the chances of doing this are eighty-six million to one. Thank you John, but no thank you.

There are a significant number of people who say they have dreamt they are going to win and then gone on to do so. On the Tuesday before the fourth National Lottery draw, a set of numbers appeared to Anne Morgan, from Colyford, Devon, in her sleep. In the morning she jotted them down and went along to enter them for the big roll-over draw. That night she was planning how to spend her £337,644 jackpot.

It's not the first time, and it won't be the last that dreams have thrown up an equally good track record. Ken Jefferson from Somerset, had not one but four premonitions about winning.

First he 'saw' his successful ticket, then he visualised receiving the cheque. This was followed by a daydream of the new house he would buy and finally he imagined the begging letters arriving.

So when the lucky numbers dropped one by one through Guinevere's hatch, Ken wasn't in the least bit surprised to be celebrating winning the jackpot.

Many people are sceptical about such stories, but the idea that you can dream the future has been gathering credibility within the scientific community. Although none of the many theories put forward about predictive dreams has been proved yet, it does appear our dreams can, and probably do, contain more information than we give them credit for.

At the end of the day, the key to winning the lottery and enjoying a stress-free, longer and happier life it seems is not dreams but positive thinking, according to leading psychic Roz.

'People who win the lottery are those who really, really, really want to win it,' she says. 'They want it so much that they get it.'

Roz, forty-seven, whose clients include solicitors, teachers, nurses, writers, policemen and criminals, believes the power of positive thought is the way to run our lives.

'I believe that nothing good is going to happen to you unless you feel good about yourself,' she says. 'I love me. I do not use or abuse myself and nobody else does. You should never waste your energy on people who are bad to you, just tell yourself they do not exist.

'Then relate that positive style of thought to the lottery. But if you start working out how you are going to spend the money before you win it, you don't deserve to win. And you won't. You can have everything – but you can't have it all at once. My belief is that it should come slowly, in a divine order. I know that I will be rich, but it will not be from winning the lottery. My wealth will be linked somehow to my talents. I am pleased about that. It is good to know that I will do it by myself, not through an act of chance. That wouldn't be satisfying to me. That's why I'll never win.

'I haven't noticed a winner yet who has been gregarious or particularly talented. People who tend to win have no other way of getting rich. It is their only chance.

'They are looking for their fifteen minutes of fame and this, sadly, is the only way they will get it.'

Superstition also comes into play in the lottery. It is a strange thing. It can govern what we do in our lives because we fear the consequences of ignoring it.

That's what young mother Cheryl Lock thought, anyway.

The story begins in January 1995, when retired cabinet-maker Alf Goldthorpe bought his first-ever National Lottery ticket. Sadly, Alf, seventy-four, collapsed and died of a heart attack fifteen hours before the draw revealed he was a £10 winner.

His granddaughter Cheryl, twenty-eight, from Mildenhall, Suffolk, decided to continue using his numbers every week in memory of him. She stuck to 7, 16, 19, 25, 26 and 28 for fourteen weeks without winning a penny. Then on the fifteenth week her numbers came up – and she won £93,706.

Said Alf's widow, Kathleen, seventy-one, 'I am sure he must have been watching over her to make her win. He would think it was hilarious. I bet he is up there somewhere having a drink to celebrate.'

So winning the lottery it seems is all about luck, positive thought and superstition.

America's leading numerologist, Ellin Dodge, has her own thoughts on winning the lottery. She believes a win will bring a love boat to freedom.

'With the help of your predictable lucky numbers the gang-plank will come down and you can step aboard,' she says. Work that out.

She urges us, 'Use the vibes and protect your energy and space. Chime to your own tune.'

According to Ellin we attract people and experiences that have the same numbers. These numbers show up in people's names, birth dates, house addresses, telephone numbers and even social security numbers.

Although it is true, in a practical sense, that social
security numbers are spewed indiscriminately from a
computer, the teachings of the ancients say that there
are no accidents and no coincidences. Life is ordered
and very much about numbers.

'We attract what is meant to be,' preaches Ellin. 'It
is a matter of deciding whether we will be open or
closed to a consciousness that uses the sensing mind
and not the physical brain.'

She goes on to tell us that numerology is a numbers
system that began with the cave people and was
known in ancient Egypt. It is included in the Indian
Vedas, the Chinese Circle of the Heavens, the Hebrew
Kabala and was part of the Phoenician and Chaldean
cultures.

Numerology's system for personal lucky numbers is
based upon the numbers that correspond with the
letters in your first name. The numbers of your birth
day, month and year are used to find your destiny. An
interaction of birth-date numbers is used to find your
best lucky number for the present time. The calendar
day lucky number – a mixture of month, day and year
– is used with your name and birth date numbers
when playing the lottery.

'When mixing the numerics of the universe with
your personal number symbols you engage the
energy coming from the media, the population as a
whole and the activity of the lottery organisation,'
says Ellin. 'Your concentrated power means that
you may be singing numerology's praises all the
way to the bank.'

She adds, 'By using numerology to find your
personal lucky numbers and coordinating your

actions to the tempo of the universal calendar numbers, you are likely to hang a framed gold record in the music room of your Mediterranean villa. However, to go for gold, it helps to have a direct route – a system.'

Got it so far? No, neither have I. But in the following pages Ellin teaches us how to calculate our personal numbers. She works out that footballer Gary Lineker's are 24, 6, 8, 32, 5 and 48; actor Mel Gibson's are 29, 2, 4, 10, 1 and 27; supermodel Cindy Crawford's are 28, 1, 2, 44, 8 and 22; and Cilla Black's are 45, 9, 4, 49, 13 and 22.

To simplify Ellin's vision, why not write down all the numbers in your life? Your house number, your birth date numbers, your age, your passport number, the numbers on your car number plate, your telephone number, your TV licence number, even the numbers of the make of your fridge. Once you have the numbers that are special only to you, mix them all up, shake them around and play the lottery. But only ever use the numbers from your life style. And use them at random. Why not?

Whether you are working out the hottest and coldest numbers in the game, picking them from supermarket bar codes or the family birthdays, one thing is certain, you still need a lot of luck. And some people seem to have more than others. Take Shaun Renaud from Bracknell, Berks.

On a cloudy Saturday in April, jobless air-conditioning fitter Shaun, thirty-two, got off to a gentle start by picking up a £7.50 payout in the Grand National. He put the money into scratch cards and guess what? He won £42. It was indeed his lucky day, so he bought twelve £1 lottery tickets – and that evening scooped £2.7 million.

Although some people are destined never to win the lottery, what about those who believe their destiny is to win?

Take Father Roberto Russo. The sixty-four-year-old Italian priest has been very much in demand ever since the people of Clerkenwell, London, discovered he had a knack of picking lucky numbers. Over the last twenty years he has quietly won more than £30,000 in church raffles, tombolas and guess-the-weight competitions. He has also won two Fiat cars, a colour television and a holiday in the Bahamas. He claims he can't remember losing a game of chance since arriving in London. But he hasn't kept a penny for himself.

'I enjoy the excitement of winning and I always hope and pray I will win something big, of course,' he says.

Now Father Russo's pastoral work has apparently taken on a new dimension.

'The telephone hasn't stopped ringing,' he says. 'People come up to me in the street asking what my National Lottery numbers are. I just tell them the first figures that pop into my head.'

Each week he spends £5 on the same numbers and has a special system. He chooses one set of numbers from the bottom of the ticket, one from the top, one in the middle and then two spread over the whole card. We may laugh, but he has already won £110 and is probably warming up for something really big.

Some of Father Russo's parishioners are addicted to betting on the horses.

'Sometimes they cry because they can't even walk past a betting shop without going in,' he says. 'But they realise their position and I give them advice. I try to convince them to play the lottery instead. The lottery is very different from the horses.'

But how's this for luck? Schoolboy Mark Stammers, from Bury St Edmunds, Suffolk, was gob-smacked after winning a prize on the lottery with a £1 coin that he had swallowed.

When X-rays showed the coin was in his stomach, everyone told him he was lucky he hadn't choked. He waited ten days for nature to take its course, then got his parents to put the lucky coin on the lottery – and won a tenner.

'We didn't dare tell the shopkeeper who sold us the ticket where the coin had been,' said his dad.

Luck, destiny and the lottery seem to be playing a part in all our lives. And nowhere more so than in the life of Julio Castillo, whose number was definitely up.

The petty thief was handed two letters in his Bolivian prison cell. One told him he had won £62,000 in the Bolivian National Lottery, 1,000 times the country's average weekly wage – and the second informed him that his appeal against the death penalty for killing a shopkeeper had been turned down. He was executed by firing squad the next day.

Chapter Seven

All Together Then!

The lottery had created a new hell – the jackpot syndicate. Two glaziers walked away with £22.59 million and within hours the public knew every skeleton in their cupboards.

As Mark Gardiner and Paul Maddison popped champagne bottles for the benefit of a posse of photographers at a roundabout on the A4145 between Watford and Rickmansworth, a bitter family feud raged. Relatives, former friends and colleagues were queuing up to denounce them.

They arrived at the back door of Camelot's lottery headquarters in Watford and began their transformation by shedding their shell-suits in the lavatory and reappearing in £140 Next outfits.

In the Camelot canteen Mark, thirty-three, was flanked by the latest woman in his life, Brenda McGill, thirty-nine, a nursing-home supervisor who, we were later to discover, was five months pregnant by him but married to another man.

Everything went well at first. It was all very light-hearted. The questions were predictable. 'How do you feel?' 'When did you realise you had won?' 'Is there one thing you have always wanted to buy?' 'Have you spoken to your bank manager yet?'

Mark declared that the win would not change his life. 'I will buy a new car,' he said.

Paul chimed in, 'We stayed up half the night to work out how to spend the money and we only got to £1 million.'

Both men intended to continue working for their glazing company and Mark joked, 'I might get a new van.'

Then came the questions they did not want to hear.

'Mark, your ex-wife has been saying unkind things about you, what do you say about that?'

'Mark, will you be contacting your adoptive mother?'

'Mark, will you be giving any money to relatives?'

The painful exchange proved too much for Camelot's Director of Communications David Rigg, who was sitting beside the winners. He wasn't pleased by the way the questioning was going.

'Mark is making it very plain that he doesn't want to talk about all this,' he said.

Unfortunately for Mr Rigg, others did. They wanted to know all about the winner who had been married three times and had allegedly left a former wife penniless.

As the press conference went on, somewhere down a telephone line Mark's former best friend was condemning him as a violent, hard-drinking womaniser. Lifeboatman André Bourdon-Pierre, thirty-two, had

128

sat next to Mark in class at Priory Road School in Hastings, East Sussex. He told how classmates had nicknamed his friend 'Oil Slick' because of his greasy hair. The friendship ended years later, André claimed, because of Mark's crazy behaviour. In 1983 he was banned from driving for a year and fined £100 after smashing up a company van in a late-night crash. He was aggressive with his family and had a serious drink problem.

André told reporters that his big regret was saving Mark's life in a work accident. 'We were working on a plate-glass window in a busy street and we had to take it out. Suddenly the glass split,' he said. 'I quickly snatched a sheet away from his back. Now I wish I never had. If the glass had dug in him, he would have been either crippled or dead. I now run a rival glass company to his and he is always trying to get one over on us.'

André didn't stop there. He told how Mark was obsessed with women. 'First of all he gives them all the charm because he has got the gift of the gab,' he said. 'But then he will dump them.'

Mark and André were apparently drinking partners before falling out. 'A typical night for him was ten pints of lager, then chasers,' André added.

Mark's adopted mother, sixty-seven-year-old Irene Cresswell, didn't have a kind word to say either. She claimed her son had terrified the family with his rough ways.

'We adopted him in 1962 and it was the worst decision I ever made,' she said. 'He was trouble for us while he was a schoolboy. All I want is the money he owes me.'

Irene told how Mark met his first wife Bridget while working in a local amusement arcade.

'He married Bridget in the Catholic church in the High Street in May 1985. But by Christmas they had parted. They were always rowing. He would go out and say he would be back at a certain time but he never was.'

Then came second wife Sue in 1988, we all heard. Irene said, 'We thought Sue was silly marrying him because we knew what he was like. A few weeks after the marriage she phoned me up about two in the morning saying, "He's not home. What shall I do?"

'He and Sue had all sorts of bust-ups. Then in 1991 he married Kim, but the first I knew of it was when his daughter was born. That man is hell on earth. I think God in heaven has done a wrong thing giving him all that money.'

The allegations and revelations dismayed Camelot. How many more people would come out of the woodwork?

Mark did not respond to the bad press, keeping a dignified silence. At least he had £11 million to anaesthetise the pain. But behind the scenes the fabric of a very sad story about his early life was beginning to emerge.

The two June jackpot winners ran Croft Glass, a double-glazing company based in Hastings, Sussex. Immediately news of their win spread, Paul, whose wife Ruth, forty, was a primary school teacher, was described as 'dislikeable' by former colleague, glazier Bob Mann.

'He can be as nice as pie one minute and then fly off

the handle at you the next,' he said.

But one of the winners' employees told a different story. Carl Paine said: 'I am pleased for them, they are good employers. I just hope this is not the end of my job. We have all been told not to come to work today.'

At the head of the queue claiming a share of the record pay-out however, was Mark Gardiner's third estranged wife, Kim, thirty-three. She told how she threw him out because of his drinking bouts and said that she was now living on £65-a-week income support with their three-year-old daughter.

She described the man she met in a Hastings pub as a 'two-faced, lying git' and 'a lying bastard'. And she complained she was never told he had a string of ex-wives and girlfriends living in the quiet seaside town.

'I deserve half of his win because he has never paid anything towards me or our daughter or the mort-gage,' she said. 'I should get some money after what I have had to put up with. I hate him. I would never have married him if I knew what he was like.'

This time Mark did speak up, 'It's all very sad,' he said. 'There are two sides to every story. When this all calms down my true friends will tell the truth about me. I just hope people aren't put off buying our windows.'

Mark changed his name after falling out with his adoptive parents, reverting to the name of his natural parents who lived in Reading. But he had no contact with them or with his adoptive parents.

Irene Cresswell said, 'I haven't seen him since he won. I don't want to. I wish he was dead. He has been nothing but a curse to this family. I adopted him as a tot in 1962 and cared for him as my own. Things started to go wrong when he was sixteen. Ever since he has been in trouble. When he got married to his second wife I refused to go into the church until he left the pub. He even missed his daughter's second birthday.'

But Mark made it clear he had no interest in healing the family rifts. 'They have got their own lives to lead,' he said. 'I am not going to contact them. I am going to let sleeping dogs lie.'

As the champagne flowed and he cuddled his new girlfriend Brenda McGill, Mark revealed that there was only one person who would be guaranteed any help from his share of the huge pay-out – his daughter by Kim, who was now seeking a divorce.

Legal experts said Kim was unlikely to get half of his fortune. A judge would probably decide that the separated wife of a lottery winner was entitled to a much smaller portion because she did nothing to help him get the cash.

Meanwhile Paul briefly took the spotlight off Mark by talking to reporters about buying a new car and a new house. His forty-year-old wife, Ruth, admitted that she disapproved of gambling and thought that he and Mark were spending too much on their weekly flutter. Their stake was between £20 and £50 a week. Then she smiled, 'I was wrong, wasn't I? I'll just have to eat my hat now. I thought it was all a total waste of money, that the likelihood of winning was too remote.'

Ruth was spending some of her share of the windfall on singing lessons.

'I've got a terrible voice,' she said. The couple, who

had been married for seven years, had two sons from Paul's previous marriage.

Though Mark failed to respond to the allegations against him, he was extremely hurt. His thirty-nine-year-old girlfriend, nursing-home assistant Brenda, said, 'He is a lovely guy. We have lived together for seven months but there are no plans to marry.'

Mark, guided by the careful hands of Camelot, mostly kept his comments strictly to the subject of his win.

'We were due to discuss our overdraft but I told our bank manager that we would not be renewing it,' he said. 'We may take on some more staff and let them fit windows while we sit in the office picking our lottery numbers.'

The pair only realised they had won when Mark went to play bowls at the local green on Sunday after the draw and remembered he had not checked his Camelot ticket.

'I recalled the first three numbers and I knew the others were in the 40s,' he said. 'But it was not until I telephoned Paul from the bowling green that we checked and realised we had hit the jackpot.'

Behind the scenes the row raged on.

Mark's second wife accused him of ten flings in their eighteen-month marriage, and told how his womanising and boozing wrecked her life. The marriage, she told the *Daily Mirror*, was in trouble from their wedding day when Mark had to be dragged out of the pub to say, 'I do.'

Sue said, 'I remember getting to the altar and smelling the alcohol on his breath. Mark was so drunk that after the reception he fell fast asleep.'

At other times, he was a chronic womaniser, she said. 'He should spend his winnings on buying himself a harem – that way he would never be bored. Marriage is obviously not for him as I learned to my cost. Mark would be happier with a slave because that is how he treated me.'

But perhaps the saddest and most disturbing aspect of the story was when another skeleton in the cupboard came out. For as if Mark wasn't hurt enough by all the allegations, someone came along to stir up the already troubled waters.

A week after his win, his real father emerged, beaming with pride from the pages of the *News of the World* and saying, 'That sounds like my boy.'

With a lager in his hand, club bouncer Dave Moppett, nicknamed The Bull, said, 'From what I have heard he is just the sort of lad I was. I like meaty, married women, I knock back ten pints a night, smoke twenty-five fags a day and yes, I admit I'm a real ladies' man.'

Sipping his pint, fifty-eight-year-old Dave marvelled at Mark's record jackpot and the tales which had come out since.

But in spite of Mark's three failed marriages and a string of mistresses, Dave boasted, 'His record on the women front is nothing compared with mine. When I got my nickname, The Bull, women chased me all over. I must be good with the ladies otherwise they wouldn't go out with me.

'Mark was born after I had a fling with his mum Glenda. She was married to some other bloke serving abroad in the RAF. Glenda was a very good-looking woman in those days.

I'M IN THE MONEY. Ever-smiling TV presenter Anthea Turner bathes in cash for a Lottery promotion. And why not … she was reported to be earning £266 a minute. *(Courtesy Express Newspapers)*

JUST LOOK AT ME NOW. Anthea Turner faced a barrage of criticism when she launched the BBC's National Lottery live show. But soon the critics were eating their words. *(Courtesy National Pictures)*

CHEERS LADS. Publican Neil Duncan and his syndicate toast their good fortune after winning the Lottery. Neil only realised that he and the lads had hit the jackpot as he stood in a queue to pick up what he thought was just £10. *(Courtesy Express Newspapers)*

GIRL IN A MILLION. Pam Hiatt put British Lottery winners in the shade when she scooped £54 million in an American draw. But the single mother knew exactly what to do about the gold diggers. 'I only date rich men – I hear that Prince Charles is free again!' she said. *(Courtesy Express Newspapers)*

A TOUCH OF GLASS. Glaziers Mark Gardiner (right) and Paul Maddison (left) celebrate scooping £22.59 million on the Lottery with their partners. But hours later their win turned sour when Mark found himself at the centre of a bitter family feud. The pair shrugged it off. 'We stayed up all night to work out how to spend the money – and only got to a million,' joked Mark. *(Courtesy Express Newspapers)*

THE CHAMPAGNE SET. Bernard O'Keefe celebrates his multi-million pound win with his family … but he would give it all away if he could get his health back. The fun-loving, father-of-two suffers from multiple sclerosis. *(Courtesy Express Newspapers)*

THAT'S MY GIRL. Happiness is a birthday cake … and £6 million for lucky winner Ken White, pictured celebrating his granddaughter Charlotte's birthday. *(Courtesy Express Newspapers)*

HERE WE GO. Anthea Turner and Gordon Kennedy get to know the Big Draw machine as they prepare for the launch of the BBC's National Lottery live show. But it was a rocky road ahead. *(Courtesy BBC)*

HERE'S TO SCOTLAND. Joyce and Jim McGurk toast their £1.3 million win and go down in history as Scotland's first Lottery millionaires. The Rolls-Royce doesn't belong to them – yet! *(Courtesy Graeme Hunter)*

'I only found out she was pregnant when someone told me she had gone to hospital for something. After I phoned up to find out what was wrong the nurse said she had given birth to a boy.

'Well, I can tell you, I was completely dumbstruck. I didn't know what to do so I just hung up. A few days later I saw Glenda in the pub. When she spotted me she ran to the back of the bar and came back with a bundle in her arms. She shoved it into my arms and said, "This is your baby." When I looked down at him I was speechless. I held him for a while and just gasped for words. Then she took him off me and I never saw him again. Her father ordered me out of the pub. And to think that was the baby who is now worth £11 million. I had him in my hands for four minutes and let him go . . .'

Dave, who lives on the tenth floor of a council tower block in Reading, added, 'Glenda's husband didn't want anything to do with looking after the baby. I later heard that Mark was adopted and after that I lost track of him. I had no idea where his adoptive parents took him.

'Over the years I did think of my little son. You do, don't you? My dearest wish now is just to see him again and say, "Hello, I'm your dad."

'I want us to go somewhere we can talk so that I can explain what really happened all those years ago. We can have a beer together and just chat. I don't want any of his money – but if he was to offer me a few quid, well, I wouldn't say no.'

The story grew sadder. For Mark might have scooped a fortune, but he would never win the love of his real mother, Glenda.

'He was a disease,' she said, recalling how his birth almost wrecked her life. 'That's how I felt when I was carrying him. And that is how I remember him even today. I call him my biological baby because there simply wasn't any loving feeling attached to the way he was conceived.'

Glenda, fifty-five, spoke out because she wanted Britain to know why she would never see Mark despite his new-found wealth.

'I just didn't love his father,' said the blonde doctor's receptionist. She had been married to husband Brian for eighteen months when she went with ex-soldier Dave. At the time, Brian, now a fifty-year-old postal worker, was doing National Service building RAF runways in the Middle East.

When Brian realised the boy wasn't his, he left Glenda. Now she can hardly remember Mark as a tot.

'I didn't like him,' she said. 'I don't think I ever kissed him, not even when I handed him over to his new adoptive family, the Cresswells.'

Glenda and Brian finally got back together and had two children of their own, who never knew about their secret half-brother. The only reminder Glenda had of son Mark was his private adoption papers, which she hid away in the loft of her home in Reading.

'I kept them in case the Cresswells came back and said they didn't want him,' she said. 'Then I'd have proof he was theirs.'

But all the pain was to return when Mark reportedly traced the family and wanted to get in touch.

'It was my worst nightmare,' said Glenda. 'Then I

feared Mark might try and buy affection – give me a million just to see me. But I honestly want nothing to do with him. I don't want a penny.

Husband Brian was not so sure. He said, 'I accept Glenda's wishes, but I have been hurt twice, once when my wife had another man's baby and again when Mark came back into our lives.

'I hope he does give me a million – so that I can take Glenda away from all this and bury it once and for all. I deserve it!'

For Mark £11 million in the bank will cushion him from the sniping, but there is something to be said for trying to keep your lottery win a secret from the start, although some people do find that difficult to do.

If you are sharing a ticket with a friend as Mark was, or you are in a bigger syndicate, experts warn you to draw up an agreement.

For syndicates who strike it lucky on the National Lottery could lose a huge chunk of their winnings to the taxman. Financial experts advise punters to draw up a formal agreement in order to avoid the dangers of paying Inheritance Tax if the ticket holder dies suddenly. At present some 'gifts' can be the subject of taxation if a sudden death occurs.

So how safe is your syndicate lottery number – and what are your rights? Imagine you are a part of a lottery syndicate and you hit the jackpot. You are rich, a millionaire overnight. But then disaster strikes. Just as you reach for the champagne, your workmate Joe Bloggs, whose name is on the winning ticket, is run over by a bus and killed on his way to the party. Bad news for Joe. But is it bad news for you? Apart from the sadness of losing your friend, what does it mean for you and the rest of your syndicate?

Rest assured, says Camelot, you and the rest of the group will still be able to pick up the cash. But if you have not drawn up a formal agreement, all syndicate members could find themselves liable to Inheritance Tax. For the Inland Revenue could tax everyone in the group if the person whose name is on the winning ticket dies within seven years of the win. So take the precaution of drawing up an agreement – preferably witnessed by a solicitor to prove that you are part of a bona-fide, lottery-playing group. That way, should the syndicate leader die, the rest of your group will not find themselves taxed on their winnings.

A Revenue spokesman said, 'People should always have some form of written agreement.'

'A verbal pact may be acceptable under law,' said David Major of accountants Touche Ross, 'but a written contract simply helps clarify everything because the Revenue has been known to take a dim view of verbal agreements in the past. It is the only sure way to prevent disputes.'

Not that there was any funny business when a Syndicate from Newport Pagnell won £1.7 million in November. The members had a verbal agreement and it was all shared out fair and square. Camelot advised them to inform the Revenue of their win straightaway, which they did. So, if your syndicate scoops a big win and you do not have anything in writing, contact the taxman immediately. Tell him your share of the win was received under a pre-existing group arrangement. Better still, get something in writing. The other very good reason for having a group contract, of course, is to stop the syndicate leader suddenly developing amnesia after a win. If your leader happens to forget being part of a group, you can remind him or her, and Camelot, with hard-written evidence.

Draw up an agreement before your group plays the lottery and write the date of the contract clearly on the front. It should show the names of all the players, the amount of money each of them contributes and the percentage share they are entitled to should you all win. State who buys the tickets and claims on behalf of the group and state what will happen if a member fails to pay his or her weekly contribution. Everyone in the group should sign the form in front of a witness, preferably a solicitor. Finally, give each of the members a copy of the agreement and keep the original in a safe place.

Not all big syndicate winners get such bad press as Mark Gardiner and Paul Maddison. For some syndicates winning has just brought joy into their lives, although it seems sometimes they simply can't get away from the recriminations.

Take sixty-four-year-old widower Fred Baker who won £220,000 as part of a syndicate, the other members of which were eight women pensioners living in the same sheltered accommodation as Fred. He, too, experienced the negative side of getting rich quick. Fred bought his daughter Julie a car and himself a new bed – but that was all. At his age, he did not hanker after many possessions.

'The only thing I haven't liked is the jealousy,' he said. 'Some people I've known for a couple of years don't even speak to me any more. I've also had people come up to me in the street and say, "You're that fat sod who won the lottery!"

'There have been some begging letters from charities too. They come in addressed to Fred Baker, Lottery Winner, Newport Pagnell. The trouble is, if you start giving away £20,000 here and £20,000 there, the money's gone before you know it.'

Fred plans a world cruise and has made a generous donation to Barnardo's.

It was in the second week of the National Lottery that he and his syndicate won £1.7 million.

'I was watching the results on TV while the girls were all at the British Legion because they like a drink and a sing-song on a Saturday night,' said the former Barnardo's boy. 'I just sat there, frozen to the spot. I rang the Legion to tell them, but the girls thought I was taking the mickey.'

Has the eligible widower had any marriage proposals from gold diggers? 'Not really,' he said. 'I would like to remarry, but you wonder if they want you or your money, don't you?'

His main joy over winning was his new, adjustable bed, that massages his back and legs.

'All the girls want to try it,' he said.

Meanwhile it was an old folk's home that claimed the title of the largest single group of jackpot winners in the National Lottery. Champagne corks were popping at the Leonard House rest home in Sunderland, where thirty-five staff picked up £38,782 each.

But there was more than champagne on tap when a pub syndicate got blotto over their lottery win. For the twenty-seven lucky punters thought they had won £10 or £20 – but instead they picked up £1.3 million, so the drinks were on the house. The bill was £1,000 for the beer (728 pints), £270 worth of whisky (one gallon) and £1,000 worth of champagne as well as half a gallon of gin and half a gallon of vodka.

Landlord Neil Duncan of the Three Postboys in Wrotham, Kent went to collect his syndicate's win at the post office, believing that he and his friends had picked five numbers correctly. As he queued he saw Saturday's winning combination displayed on a board and couldn't believe his eyes. He had all six numbers on one of the lines.

In disbelief he went home to his pub to double-check his ticket on Teletext. It was true. Within minutes he had rung Camelot who told him he had hit the jackpot.

The members who paid in most to the syndicate picked up almost £100,000 each, while the rest pocketed £30,800.

'With forty-four lines of numbers to study on the ticket it is no surprise I missed one on the winning line,' said Neil.

When Alwin Holness answered the telephone, he thought his pal was playing an April Fool's joke on him.

'Pack it in, don't be daft,' he said.

'Alwin, I'm telling you we've done it!'

Alwin put down the receiver and turned to his wife. 'Shirley, they reckon we've won £11 million!'

141

Within days Alwin was in hiding, complaining about the problems of being rich. He was sharing an £11 million win with three friends, but he was worried that his £2.78 million share would bring him a bundle of trouble.

Speaking at a secret address where his family were in hiding, Alwin, thirty-two, said, 'I know it sounds daft, but it isn't all a complete bed of roses. It has completely turned our lives upside down in a few days and we need time to think, plan and adjust. I was a factory worker on £180 a week and now I'm a millionaire. Of course I'm over the moon about the money but it's taking a bit of getting used to.'

His wife Shirley, thirty-six, who ran a pub to boost the couple's income, said, 'We like where we live and are a happy family. But I'm afraid some people might just give us a bit of trouble because of the win. I'm not saying it's jealousy or because we are a mixed marriage, but every place has its nutters and we just don't want to attract them. We are keeping out of the way for the time being to let things settle down. But we are obviously overjoyed about the money. It's changed our lives overnight, although we know it's important to keep our feet on the ground.'

Alwin and twice-married Shirley, who live in Tipton, West Midlands, have four children.

'Our five-year-old daughter is really happy at school and we really don't want to move her,' Alwin told reporters. 'But everyone in the area now knows about the lottery cash and we don't know whether that will make things different for her and for us. We were happy in our little house, we have worked hard for it and like the area. Of course we will probably move but we hope residents in the town accept us as the same people we were before the win. We are very lucky. That's the only thing that has changed. I have worked all of my life and I can't see myself just sitting around all day doing nothing. I've quit my job for the time being and I might go back for a bit again and see what it's like. Things are up in the air at the moment.'

Alwin and Shirley celebrated their good fortune with a bottle of sparkling wine at a family party before meeting fellow syndicate members to discuss plans with a Camelot financial adviser.

'The other lads do not want to be identified and I respect that,' Alwin told the press. 'We were all happy at the factory or working out down at the gym, but they have all left their jobs to sort out their futures too.'

The syndicate's ex-boss Peter Moore faced a mini-crisis at his factory, which made signposts and traffic-lights, because he lost almost a quarter of his small workforce overnight when they quit.

There was a mini crisis too for East London cabbie Gerry Konyn, who entered the same combination of numbers twice, once as part of a syndicate and again under his own name. Trouble arose with his mates, who got only £80,000 each when he won £1.37 million all to himself.

But for thirty-two supermarket check-out girls who rang up a tasty bonus when their syndicate's lottery numbers checked out, life went on as normal. The till girls matched five numbers and the bonus ball and each got £5,500 after sharing £176,432. Despite their good fortune, all those due at work the following

Monday turned up for their £4-an-hour jobs at the Tesco superstore in Baldock, Herts. The girls, who had been choosing numbers together for four weeks, bought their winning ticket at the store. As they went off to celebrate, one of their workmates said, 'They turned up today because after the money has been divided up there isn't enough to let them give up their jobs.'

Meanwhile a syndicate of security guards at trouble-torn Lloyds of London were back at work too after picking up a cheque for £416,000. While thousands of ruined Names were pinning their hopes on a rescue package the seven anonymous guards were popping champagne bottles.

Christopher Stockwell, Chairman of the Lloyds' Names Association working party, said, 'We were delighted for them. They were getting real money – something we were still waiting for.'

For a syndicate of theatre fundraisers there was bad and good news. First they lost £6,700 in Britain's biggest National Lottery syndicate bet. In November 1994, the 167 punters staked £50 each in a gamble to raise enough cash to finish building the Norwich Playhouse. The £8,850 bet netted only £1,606 – but paid off by giving the appeal nationwide publicity. Now the theatre has been awarded a National Lottery grant of £400,000. It was one of forty-nine organisations to share £15 million of lottery cash allocated by the Arts Council.

One of the most successful syndicate stories came from Bressingham, Norfolk, where a group of workmates hit the £3 million jackpot – and denied there was a rift with colleagues who missed out.

Twenty-three of the twenty-eight employees from BDR Agricultural Ltd collected £135,000 each after matching six numbers in the draw. General Manager Stephen Howlett said, 'I'm gutted about the ones who haven't won, but that's the situation. They seem to be pleased for us.'

Winners included part-time gardener and VE-Day veteran Jake Bowhill, seventy-two. The former Royal Navy gunner said he had an emotionally conflicting weekend, remembering fallen comrades – and celebrating his win.

One of the most tragic syndicate stories is that of the father who shot himself dead in April when he believed that a mistake had cost him and a friend a share of an £8 million National Lottery jackpot.

Timothy O'Brien always bought five weeks' tickets in advance for himself and a workmate and entered the same six numbers. He thought his latest batch was valid until the Saturday of the draw. In fact they had expired.

When he discovered on the Sunday that he would have had the winning numbers, Tim, described as a true Good Samaritan, believed he had let his family and his friend down. As his wife Maureen sat downstairs at their home in Liverpool, the fifty-one-year-old gun club member went up to the attic, took out his .22 pistol and shot himself dead.

Meanwhile a whole village in Oxfordshire had the feeling of destiny. It was hoping to become the luckiest place in Britain. But even if the local community in Wootton failed to hit the jackpot with the

National Lottery, it was still set for the record books. For newsagent Pat McCrorie had organised Britain's biggest syndicate with a weekly gamble of £14,000. He and his wife Maggie got together over 3,000 villagers to stake £20 each over five weeks.

A computer picked out permutations and combinations of numbers to reduce the odds of hitting the jackpot from fourteen to one to a theoretical thousand to one.

'We decided on this number of people to give us the best chance,' said Pat. 'While no one is going to win a vast fortune this way, we hope to increase our chances of picking up something. We accept that even if we win £10 million, that would only be around £3,000 each, but it is better than nothing.'

Just about everyone in the 2,500-plus population had signed up for the gamble along with outsiders who heard about the plan.

'We had people coming in the shop we had never seen before asking if they could join,' Pat added. 'It took a lot of effort and spare time to get it all together. We had to open a special bank account and get an accountant to check the money. There are photocopies of all the entries if anyone wants to check.'

The scheme did not rely on a big win but on getting lots of smaller prizes, he explained. Ironically the couple were still waiting for a lottery terminal to be installed in their shop and had to travel to near-by Oxford to buy their tickets.

'We have applied for one and we keep being told to be patient,' said Pat.

The couple set up their syndicate after hearing how similar schemes were organised in Australia.

Said a Camelot spokesman, 'It just shows how popular syndicates have become. They now account for twelve per cent of all entries. But I would hate to be the person who has to check the numbers.'

Sadly Pat's syndicate has so far failed to scoop a big win.

Lottery genius Stefan Klinceqicz has explained to us how to pull off the betting coup of the century and win the jackpot. The syndicate expert, who masterminded a lottery heist in Ireland, gave details of the military-style planning and the huge amounts of cash needed. If a team planning such a daring operation got it right, he said, the reward would be millions of pounds in tax-free profits.

'You can double your money,' he told us. 'But of course there's a risk.'

Lotteries in Australia, America and Ireland had already been hit by syndicate rings, which wait for a roll-over jackpot to run into many millions of pounds before they strike.

When Stefan hit the Irish lottery, his twenty-eight-strong syndicate bought eighty per cent of all possible winning number combinations.

A betting coup of this kind in Britain would take months of planning and would hinge on a roll-over jackpot. First, the syndicate would raise £14 million and pass it to a firm of accountants, who would bank it. Next, three or four people would hire offices in a central location in England where ticket buying would be coordinated. The team would include an accountant, a lottery expert and someone with a background in security. Pay-slips would be collected in batches from shops over a period of a week so as not to arouse suspicion. They would then be filled in at the HQ by a machine linked to a computer, because it would take up to a year to fill out every one of the 13,983,816 combinations by hand. The syndicate would then start recruiting small teams of ticket-buyers.

'You don't advertise for people. You just get them by word of mouth and you need at least 200,' said Stefan.

About fifty hotel rooms would be booked across the country and funds from the £14 million pot would be put into banks near-by for people to use as a cash point. To input fourteen million tickets on 1,000 machines would take about seven hours on each machine, or more than one hour each day.

'You choose machines where you don't get in the way of other people who are buying tickets,' Stefan added.

Once the tickets were purchased they would be taken back to the syndicate HQ and put in secure storage.

Stefan revealed, 'When you've got every single ticket, you just sit back and enjoy the show.'

But the biggest gamble for the syndicate is whether anyone else shares the jackpot. They are guaranteed massive profits if they are the only people with the winning set of numbers. But if it is a popular combination, the Sting-men could get stung themselves and face losses of millions.

If successful however, the operation would guarantee other prizes of at least £4 million, on top of the massive roll-over jackpot.

Of the fourteen million tickets, 252 would have five

matching numbers – netting £378,000. Some 13,545 would have four matching numbers winning £812,700 and 246,820 would have three matching numbers winning £2,468,200.

It was May, 1992, when Stefan and his syndicate won the Irish National Lottery. They decided to lay bets of nearly £9,000 in just two days to win the jackpot of £1,706,046.

But as their team of buyers went into action, Irish lottery bosses started to shut down the machines. The syndicate failed to buy every ticket combination but won the jackpot after managing to get eighty per cent. The heist made only £368,000 profit because two other people, outside the team, had the winning combination.

Meanwhile big-time gamblers tried to pull off a massive betting coup in our own National Lottery on January 14, 1995. But the syndicate of thirty-five Australian, Hong Kong and Malaysian businessmen lost £3 million because there were so many winners. The £20 million prize was finally shared by 133 people. Each received £122,000.

Rumours of the attempt had been sweeping the City of London the week before the roll-over draw. A Malaysian businessman who ran a bio-technology company flew to London from Sydney with a stake of £3.5 million. Blank lottery tickets were filled in using a computer programme and a high-speed printer. The syndicate reckoned that by cutting out some combinations they did not need to cover every possible number, and they proved to be right. Helpers were employed to offload bundles of slips in different parts of the country to avoid arousing suspicion.

The Malaysian flew out of London on the Saturday night flight after watching the draw on television and breathing a sigh of relief that he had all six winning numbers. But the flight to Sydney left at 9.30p.m., which meant he was unable to see the lottery update.

It was only when he touched down in Australia that he was told there were too many winners and the coup had gone wrong. Despite getting all the numbers correct and being able to claim thousands of minor prizes, the syndicate had picked up just £500,000.

'More than seventy million tickets were sold, so with the odds at fourteen million to one, we were expecting five winners, but instead we got 133,' said Camelot.

Chapter Eight

Instant Fortunes

Punters' chances of winning the lottery soared in March 1995, when the new Instants scratch-card game was launched. No one realised then that it would hook the nation.

Organisers Camelot said the £1 Instants game offered a one-in-five chance of a prize of up to £50,000 compared with one in fifty-four in the existing national draw. Little did we know that buying a scratch card was to become as common as buying a Mars bar.

It was dull and cloudy, the sort of weather that went with Kevin Hope's mood. Money was tight and he was still worried about the bills. Only the year before he and his wife and children had been thrown out of their £40,000 home for falling behind with the mortgage payments after he lost his job as a coal-delivery man. Luckily the family were rehoused by the council. It was his only piece of luck until now.

He stopped his battered old Ford Orion car outside the newsagent's and went in to buy some cigarettes – his little luxury. The man behind the counter handed him the change and, on impulse, Kevin bought one of the blue and gold scratch cards on the rack in front of him.

Minutes later he sat shaking in his car after rubbing the foil from his card with a five-pence piece. The twenty-eight-year-old father of two had won £50,000.

'When I scratched off the last box I was shaking like a leaf and ran back into the newsagent's to get it double-checked,' he said. 'He looked at it, shook my hand and told me I was a winner. I just jumped with joy and punched the air. It was too easy.'

For Kevin, wife Lindsay, twenty-four, and sons Karl, four, and sixteen-month-old Lewis, the win meant a big turnaround in their fortunes.

'When he came in shouting at me to look at the card in his hand I was frightened we had another bill that needed paying – and we didn't have any money,' said Lindsay. 'He showed me the winning ticket and I stood there in shock. We were both like that for about half an hour. Then we telephoned the number on the card to make sure it was true.

'Now we just want to enjoy ourselves without getting silly.'

Kevin and Lindsay bought a new car to replace their old Ford and booked a trip with the kids to Disneyworld. They also gave £1,000 to each of Kevin's sisters and their parents. They left the rest of the money in the bank.

The couple had no plans to move from their council house in Bodworth, Warwickshire.

'All that trouble has put me off house-buying for life,' said Kevin. 'I just bought a new TV and video – all the things I wanted. The money hasn't changed us. It just means we don't have to save for months to buy things. We splashed out on a £20 bottle of champagne the other night. When we've drunk it we can buy some more if we feel like it, without worrying.'

One man, however, wasn't splashing out on champagne after hearing about the new Instants game. He arrived at a shop in Boldon, Tyne and Wear, and bought £400 worth of cards in one go – but he ended up £500 down.

The mystery punter, who expected to land the £50,000 jackpot before flying off on a Caribbean holiday, insisted the cards were in sealed packs. Then he sat in his car outside the shop scratching his way through the tickets with his fingernails. All he got was a clutch of small wins adding up to £100 – which he promptly spent on more cards. Finally he lost the lot and, calmly drove away to catch his flight to the sunshine.

He certainly didn't have any of the luck that Lucy Cowley did. The eighteen-year-old student won £50,000 on the first Instants card she bought. Lucy popped into a village store close to her home near Basingstoke, Hampshire, to buy a can of Coke. On the spur of the moment she decided to have a crack at the game after the man in front of her in the queue bought £10 worth of tickets. The next card, which Lucy snapped up with the money she had to spare from her five-pound note, turned out to be the winner.

As Lucy toasted her win with a can of cola, sixteen-year-old Mark Aldred became the youngest person ever to win £50,000 on the Instants game.

'I had a very strange feeling when I rubbed the card,' he said. 'My heart started pounding and I felt dizzy. I was with some friends and I shouted, "I've won, I've won!" I had to look at it about twenty times before I could believe it. When I telephoned my mum she thought I was pulling her leg.'

College student Mark, from Gosport, Hampshire, went right out and bought a new mountain bike and cycles for his two younger brothers. And he promised his mother an extra-special honeymoon when she got married again later in the year.

But the win has not changed his dream ambition.

'I'm not letting it go to my head, I still want to be a funeral director,' he said.

The Instants game may have had instant appeal but it wasn't an instant success.

The launch party at London Zoo had a lot of potential, with sporting celebrities like soccer star Gary Lineker, England cricketer David Gower and athlete Sally Gunnell making guest appearances. But the game didn't come up to scratch despite its star-studded launch.

A computer breakdown left thousands of card buyers disappointed after they tried to claim prizes. Security software was to blame. Each £1 card had a security bar code which had to be swiped through a special terminal to validate it and reduce fraud. Some retailers could not activate their tickets and in other cases transactions were taking nearly a minute rather than just a couple of seconds to complete.

Unaware that problems were developing, Lineker went merrily on and joined leggy, smiling TV presenter Anthea Turner in a motorcycle publicity stunt as the post office distributed more tickets throughout Britain. Hours later 20,000 shops around the country were ordered to stop selling the cards as Camelot desperately tried to solve the problem.

It was an embarrassing repeat of the launch of the main lottery when the £10 million computer caused problems and shopkeepers complained that ticket machines had not been connected.

'Hang on to your winning ticket and keep it safe,' said Camelot. 'People will be paid.'

The National Lottery regulator OFLOT intervened for the first time since the game's conception by ordering the Camelot consortium to place adverts in national and regional newspapers explaining the problem. The unexpected mishap was overcome within twenty-four hours and the Instants were back on sale.

When the Instants were launched in Britain, around 300 million scratch cards were printed with a potential of fifty-five million winners. With a £1 billion market to be tapped into, the cards were predicted to become a bigger impulse buy than crisps. It was believed that twenty-six million people would be trying their luck, especially as there was a one-in-five chance of winning any prize.

The breakdown of the odds ranged from one in ten for winning £1 to one in 2,400,000 for the big prize of £50,000. The sale of the cards was expected to increase the lottery market by twenty-five per cent.

This meant that by the end of the lottery's first year, sales would reach around £437 million – £58 million more than the sale of Saturday night lottery tickets alone. Said a lottery insider, 'People are queuing to buy their cigarettes in Safeways and ordering two Instants from what they have left over from a fiver on the spur of the moment. The queues are also full of punters handing over £20 notes for numbers in the main draw and taking their change in Instants cards.'

The scratch game had certainly been launched at the right time. It brought a feel-good factor to a country very much in the doldrums. Just two weeks after the launch an incredible fifty million tickets had been sold and seventeen people had won the top Instants prize of £50,000, leaving more than a hundred £50,000 tickets in circulation. Think about that, in a nation of sixty million people.

But of one thing some medical experts were sure. The scratch-card game was healthier for us than the weekly draw.

Lord Mancroft said, 'I've been told that an article in a medical journal has pinpointed something called Lottery Stress Disorder which people suffer before and after the numbers come up on television.'

The peer, who was also chairman of the Drug and Alcohol Foundation, and who overcame a preference for recreational chemicals, drinking his last glass of alcohol twelve years ago, added, 'Our lottery game just has scratch cards, so no one can be afflicted by that ghastly syndrome.'

He was referring to a letter published in the *British Medical Journal* from top psychiatrist Robert Hunter, claiming that Lottery Stress Disorder was set to reach

156

epidemic proportions. Symptoms included hot, sweaty palms, shallow breathing and an increased heart rate.

He said, 'Patients initially show intense anticipatory anxiety, which builds throughout the week, then reaches a peak on Saturday night. Despite unrealistic odds, patients experience the delusional belief that great riches are about to befall them – and on this basis make extraordinary spending plans. Inevitably, after the draw, these features give way to a rapid deflation of mood and feelings of hopelessness. Relief is often sought through excess alcohol.

'Usually by Monday the patient has recovered sufficiently for the pattern to repeat itself.'

But just like the National Lottery draw, Instants soon descended to squalid mud-slinging and recriminations, with cases like £50,000 winner Carole Cartman.

A judge finally allowed her to have half the cash following a row with her former boyfriend Stefan Broniewski. He had blocked her bank account in a bitter legal battle over who owned the ticket, claiming she went back on a deal to share any winnings with him.

He alleged that the win came after he gave Carole twenty-three £1 Instants cards to scratch off at the home they shared in Nottingham. One of them was a £50 winner and Carole used some of the money to buy another ten cards, among them the contested, lucky £50,000 ticket. Then, he claimed, she threw him out of the house and kept it all for herself.

At Lincoln Crown Court the judge finally allowed twenty-four-year-old Carol to have £25,000 until a further hearing. Minutes later she told reporters, 'It's my money! I paid for the card and I scratched it! He's not entitled to any of the cash. This has just become ridiculous. The man has got very, very greedy. I'm almost beginning to regret the big win, but I'm glad I booted him out. He has shown his true colours. I won £50 the week before but he didn't take me to court over that!'

Angry Stefan had his say, 'It's not me who has got greedy and I am not the one who has shown their true colours. I think she has a nerve because when I met her she had nothing. She has lived the life of Riley with me and now she has decided to keep the lot and sod everyone else. I'm still gob-smacked.'

A few weeks later the row was settled. Carole finally agreed to give her former live-in boyfriend £13,000. But she said, 'I agreed to it to save more legal fees. I still don't believe he is entitled to a penny!'

The row of course was nothing compared to the anger of 600 Instant lottery players in Macao recently. They were all convinced they had won the first prize of $823, only to find that the tickets were printer's errors.

Meanwhile in Britain, the game organisers were quietly looking at the success of the instant lottery games in America where scratch cards were challenging the weekly televised National Lottery draw as a major earner of revenue. Sales of instant tickets in Massachusetts, which runs one of the world's largest lotteries, had risen from fifty million to 1.5 billion in ten years. In Texas, which went live with instant lottery games in 1992, an average of thirty million tickets was sold each week.

Sales of instant tickets in American states overall had gone through the roof. Instant games now accounted for seventy per cent of lottery revenue. Card themes, such as Blackjack, introduced in Texas, were expected to prove popular in Britain too, as were slot-machine-type games. Following the Texas example, about twelve types of game were likely to be on sale in Britain eventually, with a new game launched every three weeks on average.

Instant games in Texas are sold under evocative headings, including Cactus Cash, Texas Tornadough and Armadillo Dollars. The Instant Million game offered eight top prizes of $1 million at odds of 12.5 million to one. At the next level, 26,000 tickets paid $500 each, and 400,000 paid $40 apiece. Prizes continued down to $2.

But even the losers could be winners in America – and that could prove true in Britain too. For a Lottery Collectors Society has grown across the United States. The idea is the brainchild of retired printer Richard Bertrand who saw the potential of collecting lottery tickets as a hobby almost twenty-five years before anyone else.

His house contains a staggering collection of lottery memorabilia, including posters, promotional material and back-issue lottery magazines. The collection also includes tickets of every size, shape and colour. His favourite is the Massachusetts issue. 'It has the prettiest design of all,' he says.

Convinced that collecting lottery memorabilia would be big business, Bertrand and some fellow collectors formed an international club in 1988. Now there are 400 fee-paying members who receive four free lottery tickets and a monthly newsletter.

Richard explains, 'Unlike baseball cards, the instant tickets can't be duplicated. Any card bought is actually one of a kind. The fascination lies in the card's design which is not only colourful and artistic but changes frequently.'

Apparently, some collectors seek void tickets while others hunt tickets that won money but were never turned in. And, of course, there are those who simply want scratch-offs in mint condition.

But it could be very difficult collecting cards that have never been scratched off. The burning desire to find out if you have won £50,000 might prove too tempting for some and a whole collection would be wiped out in one frantic night as the deadline for claiming approached.

Who knows, in Britain lottery cards could be big business one day for auctioneers like Sotheby's and Christie's. After all, 1960 Barbie dolls in mint condition can now fetch up to £5,000 apiece.

If Britain continues to follow the lottery trends set by the other playing nations, it shouldn't be too long before it sees a TV game show linked to a scratch-card prize.

In France, scratch cards offer players an instant win and the chance to appear on a television show called *Le Millionaire* where they walk away with prizes worth up to £112,000.

Ireland has *Winning Streak*, one of the top three rated programmes, which operates on a similar principle. Its finale gives a punter the opportunity to spin the wheel which holds prizes of up to £250,000. One contestant won the top prize last Christmas.

Chapter Nine

On Top of the World

Lotteries may be news here in Britain, but they are nothing new. In 10 AD Augustus Caesar stood surrounded by a handful of senators at the top of one of the hills of Rome, staring at the waterlogged road that led down into the city. The buildings along its path were crumbling, the drainage systems were blocked, many of the walls were just piles of rubble. Rome was in a state of decay.

Like so many leaders to follow in history, Caesar was badly in need of cash to rejuvenate his country's beloved capital city. For days he and his advisers debated the crisis. Finally they found the solution – a public lottery. It worked. Slowly the roads of Rome were rebuilt.

But it wasn't until the sixteenth century that Caesar's idea took a firm grip in Europe, when, in 1520, King Francis I of France made lotteries legal. Merchants, forever chasing bigger profits, began to organise lotteries whenever they had a valuable product to dispose of. They realised that they could make more money in a draw than by selling the product to an individual. Governments across the Continent also recognised the potential tax revenue which could be made for the state and encouraged the merchants further.

Lottery fever raged so strongly, especially in Italy, than in 1528 'Lotto de Firenze' emerged as the first state-run gamble. A few years later, in Genoa, statesman Admiral Andrea Doria persuaded the government to approve a draw for the selection of five names from the 120 members of the Genoese nobility for election to the Senate. The twice-yearly drawing of the names aroused interest among the public, and soon betting became an important side issue. Half of all the money staked was given to the punters who guessed the five names correctly, the remainder was kept by the organiser of the lottery.

In 1566 lottery mania made its way across the English Channel and caught the imagination of the British. The south-east coastal towns of Hastings, Romney, Hythe and Dover all needed costly harbour repairs. The mayors sought advice from the Warden of the Cinque Ports, who in turn approached Queen Elizabeth I. She set the first English lottery wheels in motion by authorising a state game to raise money for the projects. It was launched in 1567. There were 400,000 tickets, with a top prize worth around £100,000 today. Less than fifty years later, in 1612, an English lottery was sanctioned by James I and raised the equivalent of £100,000 to meet the costs of colonists heading for America.

Although most lotteries of this period raised funds

for charities and other good causes, some lotteries were run for more dubious reasons and often people hesitated before buying tickets, fearing the outcome might be fixed. When Louis XIV of France drew the tickets for a lottery in the seventeenth century, the French nation held its breath on the day of the draw. Then the prizes were announced – 100,000 francs for Louis and smaller prizes for the Queen and the Dauphin. The people's anger was stilled only when the King graciously handed the money back saying it was all a mistake, something had gone wrong. The numbers were drawn again.

One thing, though, was evident, whether they were honest or crooked, philanthropic or profiteering, lotteries offered a reliable source of income as they do today. Hard-pressed governments could not ignore this fact and state-run lotteries began to spread throughout the world.

In Britain, however, lotteries had a rough passage. 'Lotteries exist to the utter ruin and impoverishment of many families and to the reproach of the English laws and Government,' said a bill prohibiting them which appeared towards the end of the reign of King William III in 1700. Oddly enough, King William had been fighting his Augsburg battles on the income from a lottery.

Throughout the following centuries, different British governments had different ideas. Some allowed lotteries and some outlawed them. 'Idleness, dissipation and poverty are increased, domestic comfort is destroyed, madness often created,' declared an 1808 House of Commons Committee report on the game.

By the time Noel Edmonds started counting down

the seconds to the first big draw in November 1994, there were somewhere in the region of 200 lotteries around the world, with ticket sales of over £60 billion a year – almost the equivalent of the UK workforce's total annual salary. Even in his wildest dreams, Augustus Caesar could never have realised what he was starting.

Today most of the world's lotteries are national or state run and, like the UK National Lottery, are used to boost funds to worthy causes. In Israel, a player makes a choice of six numbers from 1 to 49 to compete for the £750,000 first prize. All profits are invested in schools and sports centres. Holland offers a jackpot of £400,000 and draws are held monthly. Seventy per cent of the cash goes in prizes, with the profit going to the state for the benefit of the Dutch people. In Australia the prize money rises to £1.5 million. Players choose six numbers up to 45. Fifteen per cent of the proceeds goes to charities. The main beneficiary is the Flying Doctor Service. In America individual states run thirty-four different lotteries with the biggest ones being New York and Florida. New York can pay out a £4.6 million jackpot. Players choose six numbers from 1 to 49 and profits go to fund schools. In Florida, 25p in the pound goes to education and the prize money can be as much as £75 million. American payouts operate differently to our National Lottery. Prizes are often paid out over a period of years, much like a salary. One woman is definitely not complaining about that.

'I only date rich men. I hear Prince Charles and Prince Andrew are free again, they would suit me fine,' said Pam Hiatt.

She had left British lottery winners feeling like poor relations when she scooped £54 million in an American draw.

Jackpots around the world had been making headline news while the British were still hooked on bingo halls. But Pam's win in Florida staggered even the most ardent followers of lottery mania.

Pam, whose average income had been just £7,500 a year, bought six members of her family a car each after using the ages of her mother, two brothers and three sisters to pick the winning numbers in the 1995 June Powerball jackpot. And she planned to buy them houses too.

The twenty-six-year-old National Guard helicopter mechanic, who was studying political science and international relations, served with the American forces in the Desert Storm showdown against Saddam Hussein. She was on her way to a National Guard unit when she popped into a chain store for breakfast.

Shop assistant Martha Steward checked her ticket and told her, 'Honey, you'd better sit down, I have a very big shock for you – you're the winner!'

Pam, eight months pregnant, called her mother from the store. 'I can't believe it,' she screamed. 'It's all a dream.' Then she asked for a lift home because her legs were shaking so much she couldn't walk. For months she had been struggling to make ends meet. She had worked as a waitress and paraded around a boxing ring between rounds with her long, shapely legs dropping down from a skimpy dress to earn £60.

Within days Pam, who didn't have a boyfriend, had recovered her composure and was making big, big plans. First she booked a cruise to England to try her

luck with a couple of well-heeled men about town –
Prince Andrew and Prince Charles.

'I've devised a cunning way of making sure men are
after me and not my money,' she said. 'I'll only go out
with them if they are rich – like Charles and Andrew.'

Pam, who lived with her family in a small wooden
bungalow in Boise, refused to name the father of her
child expected in July, saying only that he was out of
her life, although they were still good friends.

Having too much cash brought its own problems.
She was originally going to buy a forest-green BMW
750i, but began to have doubts because she quite
fancied a Mercedes too.

'Perhaps I'll buy both, who knows?' she said.

When she went to buy a gold Rolex watch, the shop
assistant offered her hire purchase.

'I obviously didn't have the look of a rich woman
and yet I could have bought the whole store for cash,'
she said.

The tall, pretty blonde wouldn't be returning to
work. She had been living with her mother and
stepfather and now planned to buy herself a simple,
white, wooden house with three bedrooms and a
garden for her baby.

But she was mixed up about that too.

'Or maybe I'll buy a mansion in Dallas,' she said.
'Then all my family could live together. We could each
have our own wing.'

Pam had played the Powerball lottery for three
years, gambling £2 each week. The win would be paid
out at around £3 million a year.

But if you've got it and want to flaunt it, not
everyone believes it. When she tried to apply on the

telephone for an American Express card, Pam found she wouldn't do nicely.

'Hi, my name is Pam Hiatt and I would like to apply for an American Express card,' she said.

'Sure, can you tell me your annual income?' the Amex girl replied.

'Yes, it's three million dollars.'

'What? You gross three million dollars a year?'

'Oh no, I gross four million dollars, I get three million after tax!'

'Are you self-employed then?'

'Oh no, I haven't got a job!'

'I'm afraid I don't believe a word of what you have said, madam – and there'll be no card for you. Good day!'

Over in New York another woman was celebrating – the £250-a-week maid of Grace, Countess of Dudley. Portuguese-born Maria Viera popped open a bottle of champagne and vowed not to take orders any more. Indeed, if riches were the sole criteria for a mistress-servant relationship, it was Maria and not the widow of the third Earl of Dudley who should have been barking out instructions.

For Maria, forty-nine, had suddenly become a women of means too. She won a staggering £13 million in Lotto, the New York state lottery, making her a lot wealthier than Lady Dudley. This fact came as something of a shock to the elegant Yugoslavian-born heiress, who was unused to being upstaged by servants, as the aristocracy are.

Grace was first married to Polish Prince Stanislas Radziwill, who went on to wed President John

Kennedy's sister-in-law, Lee. In 1961 Grace became the third wife of the immensely rich Eric Dudley, father of the present earl, whose wife was former actress-cum-ballerina Maureen Swanson. Part of their honeymoon was spent in Paris with the Duke and Duchess of Windsor.

After Eric's death in 1969, Grace, now sixty-nine, settled into a suitably jet-setty life style, dividing her time between Switzerland, her home in Nassau (which came complete with its own Olympic-size swimming pool) and an apartment on New York's Fifth Avenue.

It was in New York that the penniless Maria, married with a teenage son and daughter, was employed by the Countess. She bought the Lotto ticket on her way to work from her home in downtown Queens. When her number came up she was so overwhelmed that it was several days before she plucked up enough courage to claim the prize – paid out in twenty annual instalments.

'I had to lie down to absorb the shock,' Maria confessed, before announcing that she would be dividing her time between Portugal, New York and the Caribbean. She had obviously been taking lessons from her mistress.

America has always had its share of breath-taking lottery nuggets. Take aptly-named Don and Shirley Pence from Phoenix, Arizona. The couple were very Middle America. They got up early, read the morning paper, poured coffee, kissed each other good-bye and went to work. The weekend was always spent renting a video, popping popcorn and relaxing in chairs on the porch. Shirley was a secretary for an insurance company and Don a self-employed painter. There was nothing spectacular about them – until, like National Guard Pam Hiatt, they won the $101,844,697.29 jackpot prize in Powerball, the lottery game that ran across eighteen American states.

On her way to rent her weekend video, Shirley had stopped off by chance at a Seven-to-Eleven shop to buy the ticket 8-23-32-36-41-PB-40. Within hours she and Don were famous, within days they had retired.

The flames licked the night sky, throwing a bright, warm orange light over the small American town of Chatham, Ohio. The crackle and snap of the burning wood was drowned every now and then by the sound of glass smashing on the porch as the windows were blasted out by the intense heat.

Robert Polcheck stood watching with a smile on his face as first the roof of his mansion caved in, then the stairs, then the top floor. The thirty-two-year-old American lottery winner had built the mansion himself with part of his $35 million jackpot win.

'He that giveth taketh away,' he said.

Winning the lottery had made his life hell. He had lost his friends and finally his wife when she walked out on him. He wished he had never bought the not-so-lucky ticket. To make amends he poured petrol over his expensive furniture and lit a match.

But although Robert felt winning a fortune did not bring guaranteed happiness, some winners were busy trying to scoop even more money. Take grandfather Joe Crawley who picked up $20 million (£13.5 million) in the Florida game. The sixty-six-year-old gambler's triumph came six years after moving to the sunshine state with a £2 million bonanza he had collected in the Ohio lottery. Experts say the odds against one person having two big wins like Joe's are something like a billion to one.

'I needed to win again because my Ohio payment runs out in the year 2007,' he joked. He can rest in peace now. Payouts from his latest success will take him through to the year 2013. The retired machinist celebrated in style, splashing out £3,000 to hire a Lear jet to collect the first instalment of his prize in Tallahassee. He had ignored friends who told him the odds of winning again were too great, and continued splashing out on tickets. Joe, whose wife Julie was with him to collect the first £650,000, had been buying about fifty tickets a week.

'The first win was a shock, but this was staggering,' said Joe, who lives in Boca Raton. 'Either God is with me or I'm always in the right place at the right time.'

Evelyn Weingarten, the store owner who sold Joe his tickets, said she had a premonition he was going to win. His combination was 14-16-19-28-39-48. But, laughed Joe, these were not the same numbers he had won with last time. How would he spend his money? 'There's nothing in particular I want to do with it,' he added. 'I think I'll spend a bit of time writing out cheques to my three children and grandchildren.' Joe is game to the end. He plans to keep on playing the lotteries until he dies.

The sun baked the tin roofs of the trailer park and John Dwight wound down the window of his battered Chevrolet saloon as he drove through the blistering heat to the supermarket on West 28.

'Why don't you let me fill in the card for you every week, they're always the same numbers?' said old Joe the storekeeper, taking John's lottery ticket.

'Nuh, if I change the whole routine now it may bring me bad luck!'

Every week for twenty years John had diligently used his wife's vital statistics for his entry – 42-33-40 – and paid his money at the same Connecticut store.

A few days later his wife Mabelle finally discovered diet and exercise and began to change shape. One Saturday for the first time, John loyally changed his numbers to his wife's new statistics.

That week the winning multi-million dollar jackpot figure was 42-33-40, John's old and faithful number. He would have won £10 million.

Another punter from Connecticut did a little better – but not much. He received the news that he had won a share of a $4 million pot in the State Lottery – the actual amount would be revealed on the day of the ceremony. Full of excitement, he hired a plane and flew his whole family down in style to the award ceremony, only to discover that the computer had blipped that week and there were in fact four million winners. He won a dollar!

Meanwhile in Florida, Dale Miller threw away his £6 million winning lottery ticket after it was ruined in the wash. When lottery officials told him they could still identify it, he spent a fruitless week searching the local rubbish tip at Daytona.

Barbara Springfield of Alabama was unable to claim her £367,000 from the state because her preacher husband was opposed to gambling and forbade her. It was him or the money. She chose him.

Unlucky Viola Alston was granted a divorce days before her ex-husband won a $1 million lottery jackpot. Then a Maryland court ruled that her former husband did not have to give her a cent.

One couple in America even stripped naked, hugged and made love after hearing they had won the jackpot – but it was a practical joke carried out by friends.

Some people however are just born lucky, like salesman Larry Lancefield. In fact, he claims to be the world's luckiest man.

Larry, 28, of Oklahoma, America, survived being hit by lightning and a plane crash that killed the pilot. Then he won £50,000 on a fruit machine – and the next day £200,000 on a lottery.

Nowhere, however, does the sun shine more brightly on lottery winners than in Spain, where 112 new millionaires were created just before Christmas 1994. And nowhere were people celebrating more than in a place called Happiness. For over 5,000 of its residents shared the £100 million top prize in Spain's National Lottery, known as El Gordo – or The Fat One.

It was a cloudy afternoon and the market square was unusually quiet in Barrio de Gracia, a normally bustling district of Barcelona. Grocer Teodora Adell, fed up with the lack of trade that day, called his brother Silvano over to his stall.

'I have an idea that will change our lives,' he said.

'Not another of your dreams, Teodora!'

'Don't make fun of me, Silvano, listen to this.'

Ten minutes later Silvano was convinced. The next day the two grocer brothers invested £5,000 of their savings in lottery tickets, each costing £150. Then they sold shares to their customers at 40p a time.

On the night of the big draw, Spain held its breath. Twenty-four children from the St Ildesfonso Orphanage in Madrid sang out the winning numbers on the TV screen. When the Adell brothers' number 49595 scooped the £100 million jackpot prize the live studio audience went wild. And in Barrio de Gracia, which means 'happiness' or 'fun' in Spanish, Teodora and Silvano's customers kissed, hugged and danced in the market square. Everyone who invested won a minimum of £4,000 and many got much more. Then it was revealed that others had benefited from the brothers' gamble in the world's biggest lottery, which paid out a total of £776 million in 1991. For the Adells had also sent tickets worth a staggering £1.5 million in prize money to dozens of friends and relatives across Spain.

A huge party was planned in Barrio de Gracia and among the guests were the twenty-four children from St Ildesfonso Orphanage. But it wasn't just the Adells and their friends who were celebrating. Other Barcelona winners claimed some £250 million in prizes and in Valencia, customers at one bar were sharing the £40.8 million second prize. Production stopped at the Bilbao plant of Siemens' multi-national electronics company after the 100-strong workforce learned they had won the £9 million third prize.

In Madrid, the administrator of a secondary school bought eighty tickets of the fourth winning number and made £1.2 million for himself and seventy colleagues. Meanwhile a pensioner only told his wife that he had invested £15 after winning £150,000 from El Gordo.

'She would have had a go at me about wasting money if she had known,' he said. 'But now she's all smiles.'

Hours later a street cleaner in Malaga announced he would be laying down his broom after winning £150,000.

A lottery official said, 'We've never known El Gordo to have been so widely shared throughout the country.'

More than £1.2 billion was staked on El Gordo, which had been running in Spain for more than 180 years. The year before, the jackpot was shared by an entire village after residents clubbed together to buy one of the 66,000 numbers outright.

In Spain, most people spend an average £150 for a share in one of the lottery numbers and the chances of winning the jackpot are one in 65,000.

Spain's ball selection ceremony has remained unchanged for decades, with orphans shouting out the winning numbers. The event, once a year in December, takes nearly four hours to complete. The tickets are beautifully designed so that they become collectors' items over a period of time – and, like American collector Richard Bertrand, some believe that one day they could be sold for a few hundred pounds at auction. They go on sale in September and people are free to buy just a fraction of a ticket from a seller. For example, one-tenth of a ticket will give you one-tenth of the prize. You can even buy one-fiftieth of a ticket.

El Gordo organisers never reveal the identity of winners and the governing organisation will not even confirm their names if they do become known. But the lottery office does release details of where the winning ticket is sold and so it is easy to find out who has won. However, the limelight can still be avoided. In November 1994, a poor immigrant worker from West Africa scooped an incredible £11.7 million in the game. Within hours the resort of Calello on the Costa Brava, where he had made his bet, was under siege by the media.

But his name, reportedly Mebba Ellah, did not come out for days. And when it did there was no trace of him. He had slipped away and deposited his cheque at a bank elsewhere in Spain. The lottery organisation later confirmed he had collected his winnings and that he wanted to donate most of it to build homes for immigrants. His whereabouts remained a secret. To this day there is no record of the homes being built.

Two Britons won more than £1 million in Spain's National Lottery in April 1993. The bonanza came six years after Eldorado bar owners Anne and Bill Blake were left penniless in a property fraud. A fellow Briton conned them out of their life savings and the couple, who left their home in Manchester in 1986 for a life in the sun, faced a desperate struggle to make ends meet.

After their win they drank their bar in the resort town of Calpe, near Benidorm, dry of champagne. With them was their German friend Barbel Thaising, who shared the £2.2 million win. He had helped to pay for the £3 lottery ticket.

The couple were choked by their success and had no

idea what to do with the money.

'It was all a bit overwhelming and I was stunned,' forty-seven-year-old Anne recalled. 'When my husband told me I had won I didn't say anything at all. I just sat down and cried. We had been buying tickets in the lottery ever since we arrived in Spain but we had never thought about winning.'

Ann and Bill just didn't know what to do with their money at first. But one thing was for sure – Anne would never cook another meal.

'I've been slaving away in the pub kitchen for six years – enough is enough,' she said. 'Now I don't even have to cook breakfast.'

Anne spoiled herself with her windfall. 'My only jewels were zircons before,' she laughed. 'Now I buy real diamonds. We had a lot of bank managers on the telephone immediately after our win. But we just let things calm down before making any major decisions about investments.'

Bill, fifty-three, vowed that life would go on as normal. 'We had a holiday in Morocco and kept the bar on but didn't run it ourselves,' he said. 'What did I do with the money? Counted it!'

The winning trio toasted town mayor José Guerras, who ran the lottery.

'They came round with champagne and twenty of us had a great party,' he said. 'They were all very, very happy. It's the first time anyone has won a big prize here.'

The Spanish lottery raises millions of pounds each year for worthy causes. Amongst the beneficiaries in 1992 were the Red Cross, the Expo fair in Seville and the Olympic Games. The Spanish Treasury and running costs swallow up thirty per cent, but the rest goes to prize-winners and worthy causes. The draw is hugely popular and Bill had some detailed advice for anyone thinking of entering the British lottery.

'Just buy a ticket. You can't go wrong,' he said.

Lotteries around the world are riddled with weird and wonderful stories, and Britain has a long way to go yet to beat them.

In America, a psychic is currently being sued for $2 million dollars after the numbers she gave a client for $50,000 failed to come up. Meanwhile in Germany a habitual criminal from Oldenburg was released from court because he had scooped £1.3 million in the big draw. The judge felt the fortune would give him a chance to go straight and reintegrate into society. Also in Germany, neighbours living in the same street as multi-million-pound winners will now get £1,200 in the lottery – so that they don't make prize-winners' lives hell. One German winner, however, stunned the nation when he revealed what he was going to do with his £3 million. The town hall worker from Essen was buying a new house so that he could get a room big enough for his toy train set.

A £12 million lottery jackpot sent the German nation into a gambling frenzy in September 1994. About forty million people, half the population, were queuing up at local lottery outlets to invest in their dreams.

Tabloid newspapers calculated exactly how much the super-jackpot of DM35 million could buy the winner: 27 luxury villas in Frankfurt; 8,098 transatlantic crossings at the normal airfare or 7 Leopard combat tanks, with enough left over for 923,493 cheesecakes.

Lottery fever had spread to Austria and the border crossing in Bavaria was blocked with cars and busloads of people determined to fill in their tickets before the Saturday draw. Burglars in Erfurt cracked open a safe and stole 666 blank lottery forms – but no one could quite understand why.

Restaurants installed TV sets and offered special lottery dinners, promising they would be served by the time of the big draw. Indigestion was guaranteed for millions of punters.

The jackpot had swollen to £12 million because there had not been a winner for nine weeks. The successful ticket had to secure the correct six numbers out of a possible forty-nine, and an additional 'super number'. The chances of winning were one in 140 million. But that did not dull the confidence of the punters. In the end a mystery man scooped the prize and he was never heard of again.

Lotteries are big business in Germany. About half the pot goes in tax-free prizes and the rest in profit, administration costs and a 16.6 per cent tax to the federal government. But the winners have to be careful; many of the 3,900 lottery millionaires have found themselves in trouble with the taxman. About half the interest earned on the jackpot is taxed and attempts to give away money are also often penalised.

On the French Riviera police swooped on a ring of faith healers who were taking money to cure impotence – and selling advice on how to win the national jackpot.

In Australia Terry Milner discovered that life was a lottery a few days after buying his fiancée a block of

big draw tickets. When Helen Borton failed to turn up
for their wedding, Terry raced to her flat in Mel-
bourne – only to find all her clothes missing. A note
explained that the tickets had won her £3 million and
she didn't want to be his wife after all. There was no
point in his following her – because she would be
half-way round the world by the time he read the
letter.

In Russia, winning the jackpot can make you a
trillionaire – but before you rush out to the travel
agent and book a flight to Moscow, remember that a
trillion roubles is worth just £160. And you should also
remember that the Russians are flying to Britain in
droves to take part in our lottery. Those who can't get
over are sending hundreds of pounds to relatives to
buy tickets on their behalf.

The lottery is also hot news in Brazil, but tempers
are even hotter. A mother of seven burned a £35,000
winning ticket after a preacher told her she would die
in a plane crash and go to hell if she took the money.
Members of her evangelical group in the city of
Fortaleza chanted, 'Burn, burn, burn!' Finally cleaner
Maria Benoize Nascimento, thirty-nine, forfeited her
prize. But when her husband found out he beat her up
and left home for good.

Brazilian congressman Joao Alves won the
National Lottery an incredible fifty-six times in 1993,
raking in £900,000. A committee is now investigating
claims that he used public funds to buy 964 tickets.

But Italy provides one of the most memorable
lottery stories – and there is a moral in it somewhere.

It was a baking hot day and Professor Vinicio Sabbatucci was sweating as he struggled to change his punctured car tyre on the motorway. He was thankful when a Good Samaritan pulled over on to the hard shoulder and gave him a hand. Soon the professor was waving the man goodbye; if only everyone could be that kind. He mopped his brow and went to close the boot. But something was missing – his suitcase. The man had stolen it. The professor was distraught.

By the roadside, where the 'Good Samaritan' had been kneeling, however, was a lottery ticket. The professor stuffed it in his pocket before driving home to Ascoll in eastern Italy.

The next day, he checked the lottery results on TV and, uncrumpling the ticket, realised it was a £25,000 winner. That same day he claimed the prize.

But then began a battle with his conscience. Eventually, he decided he could not keep the money, despite having been robbed. So he advertised in newspapers and on the radio.

'I'm trying to find the man who robbed me,' he told everyone. 'I have £25,000 for him from a lottery win. If he sees or hears my message he should contact me. I guarantee not to reveal his name.'

Professor Sabbatucci, fifty-eight, received hundreds of telephone calls from people hoping to trick him. But there was one voice he recognised – and he arranged to meet the man in a park. The robber, a thirty-five-year-old unemployed father of two, gave back the suitcase and burst into tears. He could not believe what was happening.

'Why didn't you keep the money?' he asked.

'I couldn't, it's not mine,' the professor replied.

Then he walked off, spurning the thief's offer of a reward.

If there is ever an award for extreme patience then a wife in Florida would be a runaway winner. She scooped an £11 million jackpot, hid her ticket for four months and told no one about her luck as baffled organisers hunted for the winner.

Then on Christmas morning, forty-three-year-old Johnnie Mosley gave her husband a kiss, handed him a copy of the ticket and said, 'I'm afraid this is the best I can do this year. I love you.'

When her amazed husband, Charles, recovered, he blurted out, 'But I only wanted a pair of socks!'

The Mosley's fifteen-year-old son, Mike said, 'My dad thought it was a joke at first, but when my mother told him it wasn't – that she had the real ticket in a safe deposit box – everyone started jumping up and down. Then my dad started crying. We all started crying and just danced around the room.'

After presenting the ticket to the lottery officials Johnnie said, 'We were happy before all this. This is just the icing on the cake.'

The couple pick up over £500,000 annually for twenty years. But the way Johnnie, a hair-stylist, contained herself and carried on working at her salon without letting on, amazed everyone. She also secretly kept newspaper clippings telling the story of the unclaimed fortune that was the talk of Florida. She gave them to her husband along with the ticket. State lottery officials had believed no one was ever going to claim the jackpot.

‘We've never had anyone wait so long on purpose,’ said a spokesman. ‘We are staggered how she could contain herself.’

Retired serviceman Charles said, ‘I burst out crying when she told me. But her love is worth more than all the money.’

Meanwhile, life in one small American town will never quite be the same again. When you enter Fond Du Lac, it looks unexceptional. Quaint houses line Main Street and people go about their business keeping themselves to themselves. But they call it ‘Miracle Mile’, for this is the small Wisconsin town that just can't stop winning the state lottery. A sign on the road leading into Main Street says, ‘$160 million won (so far).’

And even that is being updated, because factory worker John Staninecz has won £6.5 million. He is the fourth person since 1990 to win the jackpot with a ticket from South Main Street.

The street's reputation for making millionaires attracts buyers from thousands of miles around. When the jackpot soared to $111 million in July 1993, people came from across America, Canada and even Europe. Sure enough, the winning ticket was purchased there – at a supermarket.

Only four shops sell lottery tickets on Main Street and three of them have notched up multi-million dollar winners.

‘We will be next,’ said Tommy Reines, manager of the remaining Kwik Trip convenience store. It had snared a $100,000 winner during 1994, but was still waiting for its first multi-millionaire.

When the lottery jackpot is below $20,000 there is hardly any excitement, as if this town of farmers and cheese makers couldn't care less. But when the pot soars above $50 million, lottery fever strikes.

'We've had so many big winners, we have stopped counting the small winners who just take home $100,000,' joked tour bureau spokeswoman, Joanna Ward. 'But none of our winners has ever left town.'

Leslie Robins, America's biggest lottery winner split his £74 million with his fiancée, nurse Colleen Devries. He has stayed in town. But Colleen broke off their relationship and moved, taking £37 million with her.

A judge ruled that the £74 million pay-out could be split between the couple. 'It was always just our ticket, both of ours,' said Colleen.

They received their first, separate cheques in August 1993 in Wisconsin. A court in Madison gave the go-ahead for each of them to receive £1.2 million a year after taxes, for the next twenty years.

Wisconsin state law does not allow jackpots to go to anyone but a ticket holder without a court order. Leslie, thirty, and Colleen told the judge that they wanted to share the winnings as they shared credit cards and bank accounts.

Things weren't so friendly between another couple, however. Charles Morris, who won £2.25 million, had to give nearly half of it to the wife he had split from thirty-five years earlier. An appeals court ordered him to share his jackpot with Mercedes Thomas, who reverted to her maiden name when they separated after only two years together.

It ruled that despite their separation, the couple

were still married and she was entitled to the cash. Charles said he had tried to divorce his wife once, but she wouldn't agree and he couldn't afford the legal fees for a court battle.

'In hindsight I should have taken out a loan,' said Charles, fifty-three, from Illinois.

Mercedes said, 'I've been through the mud with this guy. He promised we would have a nice house and trips to Hawaii one day, but one day never came.'

She gets forty per cent of Charles' win, almost £1 million paid out over twenty years.

The rain poured down and people scurried up and down the street clutching umbrellas or holding newspapers over their heads. The moon threw shadows over the glistening shop doorways where some had taken shelter in the small town about twenty miles south of Rome. Everyone was talking about the weather, about being late getting home, about feeling wet. Everyone that is except Mario Afronso.

The sixty-two-year-old tramp was shuffling from doorway to doorway begging for money. Finally the police took him away just as the rain began to subside.

At the police station they emptied out the pockets of his old, shabby and torn raincoat and unwrapped a crumpled piece of paper – it was a cheque for £2.5 million. The lottery win he had never banked.

Who wants to be a millionaire? We all do – don't we? But how many of us could keep it a secret like Johnnie or Mario? Most of us would agree that if we won the jackpot it would definitely change our lives. How many times have we scoffed when we've heard winners predict that their good fortune wouldn't alter anything. But for some people it very obviously doesn't.

Maura Websdale was living with her husband and twelve children in a three-bedroomed council house when she won £500,000 in the Irish lottery. She considered adding an extension to her home, but refused to move because she liked the area. France's biggest winner, eighty-three-year-old Marie-Theresa Barre, gave away all her £10 million jackpot win, dividing it between her children and grandchildren. And in Germany a ninety-one-year-old winner redistributed his £1 million, saying it had come too late in his life for him to enjoy it.

Others were equally unenthusiastic about their riches. One forty-year-old Dubliner discovered his £1.5 million lottery prize only when he casually read his numbers in the newspaper while travelling on the bus days after the big draw. And in 1992, a fellow Dubliner was so cool about his win that he sparked a media hunt for the missing millionaire. He came forward two weeks later, having spent his time visiting banks to talk about the best interest rates without telling managers why.

There are some punters in the world who are not so cool and literally do not survive the excitement of their big win. Take for instance, Clarence Austin, who was so pleased with scooping £166,000 in a lottery in West Virginia that he burst out laughing, collapsed and died.

The excitement also proved too much for seventy-two-year-old James Smith, from Virginia, when he won a share of a £4.2 million jackpot. He leapt in the air and screamed with joy. Twenty-four hours later he suffered a heart attack, collapsed and died.

Then there was the Spanish family whose celebrations over a £250,000 win in Barcelona ended when a brother stabbed his teenage sister to death during an argument about the share-out. Seconds later he threw himself from a balcony and nearly died.

Chapter Ten

Your Number's Up!

At eight o'clock on a Saturday night, as the nation holds its breath, Merlin spins the magic balls, Anthea Turner shouts out the winning numbers and crime comes almost to a standstill. For among the most compulsive gamblers in the National Lottery are burglars, it seems.

Police forces across Britain have reported a huge drop in break-ins and other offences when Anthea flashes her smile in front of the cameras. The rise in Saturday night TV viewing for the big draw means that the housebreakers are staying home.

'At first we were a bit bewildered, but it actually makes perfect sense,' said an officer. 'Not only do the criminals play the lottery, but burglars know people are going to be watching the box in nearly every house in the land.'

Unfortunately, once the draw is over the crime figures suddenly pick up again. 'The criminals carry on as normal because they haven't won a fortune and a lot of punters go out to drown their sorrows, leaving their homes unattended,' the officer added.

With the burglars glued to their television screens, one Tory MP was quick to offer us her thoughts on what they should be watching. She called for public floggings to coincide with the big draw on Saturday nights. Criminals should get six of the best before millions of peak-time viewers as a deterrent to other thugs, said Elizabeth Peacock, MP for Batley and Spen in West Yorkshire.

'Flogging criminals live on television before or after the National Lottery will create a great impact on other villains who go out armed with guns or commit violent crimes all for the sake of a few pence,' she added. 'The punishment should be done in public as a humiliation . . . and the lottery has a very big audience to reach.'

Mrs Peacock, who supported the reintroduction of the death penalty and wanted to bring back the birch, went on, 'As I see from my postbag there is a very strong feeling that criminals should be treated tougher and so they must be seen to be treated tougher.'

Camelot was quick to react. A spokesman said, 'It is her own opinion and we have nothing to do with that.'

Before the launch of the National Lottery police were warned that its arrival could lead to a significant increase in armed robbery. The ready availability of large sums of cash at newsagents' up and down the country was bound to encourage opportunistic crime, they said.

Commander Bill Griffiths, who had responsibility for crime in the Metropolitan Police's south-east area,

assured us that strategies were in place to deal with
an increase in armed robberies.

The police began to advise banks, building societies,
post offices and betting shops on how they should
protect themselves.

Camelot was quickly expanding the lottery payment outlets to 40,000. One pound tickets were going
on sale at Tesco, Sainsbury, Safeway, Asda, Gateway
and Somerfield, W.H. Smith, Woolworths, Menzies,
Kwicksave, the Co-op and even Thresher off-licences.
Shell and Esso petrol stations would also take part,
but the bulk of the 10,000 outlets up and running
were the independently-owned shops and newsagents',
and they could be an easy target for the raiders.

B ut now another fear was growing – kidnap and
blackmail attempts against the big winners.
Camelot and Scotland Yard detectives got together in
secret talks to work out a strategy to protect the new
millionaires. Plans included a change of identity,
moving winners to new homes in different parts of the
country and high-tech security surveillance systems.
Teams from Camelot would go in and clear out the
winner's house overnight – and no one would be able
to find him or her, not even relatives, although
messages would be passed on.

In the back of everyone's minds was the launch of
the Australian lottery when an eight-year-old child of
one of the first winners was kidnapped and murdered
by a gang.

As the police issued their warnings, sad Simon
Barclay was spending six hours in police cells for a
lottery crime he did not commit.

His friends forged a ticket to trick him into thinking he was one of two winners sharing that week's £13 million prize. Simon was so excited he rushed off to the Hertfordshire headquarters of Camelot to claim his windfall – but all he got was a lot of grief. They accused him of fraud and called in the police, who took him away.

It was only as he miserably sat in the cells that it began to dawn on him that he did not remember picking the correct numbers. Police officers telephoned his shame-faced friends and they admitted they had pulled a switch on Simon as he slept. They had bought a ticket on Sunday with the winning numbers from Saturday and used sandpaper and a pen to change the date. Then they switched it with Simon's current ticket before he checked it on the Monday.

Jobless salesman Simon recalled, 'For an hour I thought I was going to be a multi-millionaire. I was totally taken in. I fell for it hook, line and sinker. The b******s! I spent six hours at Watford nick. Thank God the police were laughing at me in the end.'

Crime and the lottery soon became a focus for TV. Presenter Anthea Turner joined forces with the police in a bid to trap a conman. The *National Lottery Live* show was featured in a *Crimewatch*-style video of a crook celebrating a £53,000 win. He handed over a forged cheque from Camelot to building society staff. He had changed the amount on his real, £74 winning cheque into £53,000, then paid it into an account he had just opened at the building society in North London.

Ex-Scotland Yard man Neil Dicket, head of security

for Camelot, said, 'It was a very professional forgery. But we have a system whereby all prize cheques are compared with our records before being honoured. And of course, we never honoured this one.

'The man was caught on the building society's security video and the police issued his picture to forces around the country. It was a well-planned attempt and the most determined effort we have had to face so far.'

Neil's crack team of former detectives had by now foiled an astonishing array of frauds. The most popular trick was to present a line of winning numbers with a forged date, often with a bizarre excuse for any damage to the ticket. One couple claimed their baby had chewed up their jackpot token. Another would-be winner said the family's dog bit off the date. And yet another said the ticket was mangled in the washing machine.

Neil added, 'Blaming the child was a bit silly – it must have been a very clever baby to accidentally chew all the identifying marks off a ticket and leave the rest.'

Within weeks of the launch of the Instants game Camelot was probing an alleged swindle. Special investigators believed as many as four newsagents were selling scratch cards knowing they were non-winners. They were alerted after customers at one store complained their cards had been tampered with.

It was claimed that the fraud involved scratching off part of the card to reveal a four-digit code which the agent was then able to swipe through the lottery computer. The computer would reveal if the card was a winner or not. One newsagent investigated by

Camelot had his lottery equipment confiscated.

He was allegedly scratching off the code as soon as he received the cards. Camelot believed he then swiped them, cashed any big winners through a relative – and sold only no-win cards to customers.

'We had been waiting for crooks to target the scratch cards,' said Camelot. 'We were standing by to come down on them like a ton of bricks. This was the first suspected case, but we were sure it wouldn't be the last.'

Instants players scratch off the face of cards to reveal amounts of cash. Three of a kind mean a win. The newsagent had been supplied with 4,000 cards and sold at least 1,600. But customers at his store became suspicious when nobody appeared to win a decent prize.

Camelot was alerted and security staff secretly bought cards from the shop which showed signs of being tampered with. The investigators swooped on the owner in the first raid of its kind. They seized his lottery computer and, despite his protests, hundreds of scratch cards. They also removed his lottery advertising signs.

Later, one of the investigators passed a file on the case to the local CID.

He revealed, 'It seemed this man was swindling ordinary people out of their stake money. Customers had apparently been sold cards which the agent knew had no chance of winning because he had abused our computer by checking them before he sold them.

'We want to make it clear to everyone that the lottery is completely clean and decent. This shop may not be the only one where a fiddle is being operated. Others should be warned that we are scrutinising them very carefully.'

There was anger from the newsagent's customers.

The worst side of lottery mania took over. Angry punters besieged the shop as the newsagent hid upstairs and the police were called in to protect him. The shop was pelted with stones, the front door was kicked in and there were shouts of racial abuse. The man's Volvo car was smashed with a brick, a teenager took pot shots at his satellite dish with an airgun and a large lottery symbol was painted over the shop door saying, 'It's Not You!'

Camelot was facing compensation claims. A spokesman said, 'We will consider compensation if people can prove they bought cards from someone selling them fraudulently.'

A few months later a newsagent who swindled customers by fiddling scratchards was fined £5,000 by Liverpool magistrates.

Parmjit Singh Gill, forty-one, pocketed cash from winning Instants and sold the duds.

The father-of-four's case caused so much outrage that he left court wearing a motorcycle crash helmet so that people would not recognise him and his daughter was forced to change schools because of taunts from other children.

He admitted two specimen charges of obtaining money by deception and asked for eight other offences to be taken into consideration. He was ordered to pay £35 costs and £1 compensation each to three customers. A Camelot spokesman said: ' He is no longer a National Lottery retailer – and never will be!'

Camelot had spent hundreds of thousands of pounds trying to make sure crooks couldn't fiddle the Instants game. They looked at all the computer security systems around the world and selected the best they could find. Meanwhile a warning alerting players to the possibility of fraud was to be printed on the next scratch-card game. The move followed a second fraud in a month in which some retailers were repeatedly claiming prizes on the same winning tickets.

A spokesman for OFLOT, the lottery regulator, said that it hoped the warning would discourage retailers from tampering with cards by removing the latex covering on security code numbers in an attempt to keep the winning tickets for themselves.

'It will say something like, "Please make sure that this scratch card is intact before purchase,"' the spokesman added.

The new fraud involved only twelve of the 20,000 retailers selling Instants, said Camelot.

Cheats added an extra slice of chance to the National Lottery earlier in January 1995, when it was revealed that three bogus outlets were allegedly selling worthless tickets, printed on stolen machines. Six stolen printers were said to be circulating in Scotland, allowing shopkeepers to make large sums from selling fake tickets.

The *Scottish Sunday Mail* newspaper alleged that at least three of the machines were already operating. It claimed to have bought an official ticket dispenser for £100 in a pub car park. The seller reportedly said retailers could sell thousands of tickets a week. But as the machines were not connected to the main lottery computer, the tickets could never win.

Shopkeepers would pay out on small prizes the seller advised – but if a jackpot was claimed, the retailer would have to 'clear out quick'.

Stolen machines allowed an outlet to keep all the takings and not just the five per cent retailers officially receive.

At the end of May 1995, lottery chiefs also vowed to crack down on shops selling tickets to youngsters under sixteen. 'Any retailer caught breaking the law will have its lottery contract terminated,' said Camelot.

The move came after an undercover survey found shops selling to children as young as twelve.

Even before the big draw was launched detectives were investigating a suspected lottery fraud. Scotland Yard was called in after newsagents received an official-looking document entitled 'National Lottery (Sites) Register application form'. They were asked to return it with a £25 registration fee and an undertaking to conform to specified conditions if they wanted to sell tickets. The London address given was the base for a forwarding service for people who rented out mail boxes. In this case a mystery client had paid £47 to rent a box for three months. But the Director General of the National Lottery had not issued any literature.

One man meanwhile was accusing Camelot of trickery and was taking the lottery company to court, claiming it was misleading punters over their chances of winning.

Arthur Coward, fifty-one, had failed to win a penny despite spending £110 a week for six weeks. Camelot's promotion literature claimed gamblers had a 57-to-1 chance of winning the smallest prize of £10. But Arthur said the true odds were really 1,132 to 1. He was suing Camelot for the return of £500 of his stake.

'I know I'm the little man up against a large organisation, but I believe I'm right and I'm prepared to take them on,' said Arthur, who ran a chain of factory shops and drove a Robin Reliant van.

'I am not doing it for any personal gain. I'm not really bothered if I don't get my money back. I don't want to knock anybody who has a weekly flutter and dreams of winning a fortune. But if punters knew the correct odds against them I don't think many of them would bother buying tickets.'

Arthur, from Wombwell, near Barnsley, South Yorkshire, added, 'I paid the amount of money I did because it should have doubled my chances of winning. I have been playing with odds all my life so I know what I'm doing. After I failed to win a penny for six weeks I began to think something was wrong. Then a bookmaker friend told me Camelot was not quoting the proper odds. We sat down and worked out the real ones. I wrote to Camelot asking for my stake money back but got nowhere. I felt so angry I decided to take them to court.'

Arthur says statisticians back his findings, but Anthony Atkinson, Professor of Statistics at the London School of Economics, said, 'I will be very interested to hear the mathematical calculations that put the odds of winning at more than 1,000 to 1. I believe Camelot are right to make their claim.'

Meanwhile Camelot brought in a super-secure paper shredder to beat scratch-card fraud – nicknamed Agent 009. The fiddle-proof machine, kept in a seven-foot-high steel cage, with strictly-controlled access, would grind to dust unsold and damaged tickets.

But not all crooks are clever. Take Robert Lane. He thought he was dead lucky after breaking into a store and stealing thirty lottery tickets in Massachusetts. One of them won £2 million in the draw a few days later. When he went in and tried to collect his fortune he was arrested, convicted and jailed.

There was an abrupt end too for car-crazy Darren Vowell. The twenty-three-year-old plasterer couldn't believe his luck when he picked up £25,000 on an Instants card in May. The excited winner, who was under a driving ban after being found guilty of fifteen offences, told newsmen he would be splashing out on a luxury car. Police kept watch on him and picked him up as he drove out of a showroom in his new Mercedes. Magistrates confiscated the car, fined him £1,000, put him on probation and banned him from driving for a further eighteen months. The Mercedes Benz was ordered to be sold and the money raised treated as a fine and handed to the Exchequer.

Said Darren, 'I would rather have gone to prison than lose the car.'

Chapter Eleven

Where Your Money Went

Hundreds of potatoes were laid out along the table. But these were no ordinary potatoes and no one was allowed to eat them. These were potatoes with an electrifying message. More than 500 pounds of them were connected by wires linked to a meter that merrily ticked away. The meter, as you would have guessed (or perhaps not) was recording the amount of energy they produced.

Artist Victor Grippo was proud of his work and expected it to grip the imagination of the public and dignitaries alike. But in life, or in Victor parlance, lifeforce, things don't always turn out the way you expect them to.

The creative Argentinian was staging his first major exhibition at the Ikon Art Gallery, in Ladywood, Birmingham. He spent three weeks toiling away with his meaningful sculptures, which also included a trowel stuck in cement and a line of plates on a table.

When the people of Ladywood learned that their community was to receive £100,000 from the National Lottery funds, a long list of worthy causes sprang to mind. The critics weren't happy. With unemployment in the district running at twice the national average the money could have been used to alleviate any number of social problems. Cash-strapped hospitals would surely have been delighted to receive a gift of life-saving equipment and the money would have boosted the new swimming pool project. It went however to the controversial art gallery displaying 500 pounds of potatoes in the bizarre exhibition. For anyone struggling to appreciate the aesthetics of Victor's work, it symbolised the hidden resources in people. But local Tories claimed it symbolised nothing more than a misuse of public money.

'What a waste,' said councillor Ken Hardeman. 'How can anyone see this as art? These potatoes should be handed over to homeless organisations and put to some practical use. Like eating!'

A fellow councillor added, 'How can the public be supporting ideas like this when we are constantly hearing of spending cuts?'

The lottery cash awarded to the Ikon Art Gallery, which received another £438,000 a year in public funding, came through the Arts Council.

Gallery Director, Elizabeth McGregor, excitedly explained, 'Victor set the potatoes up as he wanted them but we have to change them over all the time because they lose their power to give off energy. It is a great coup for us to stage the exhibition. It has had a tremendous public reaction.'

The Ikon was no stranger to public reaction – much

of it adverse. It had aroused controversy in the past by exhibiting rotting fruit, piles of hay, cotton buds and a ball of string. There was even more criticism though, when people crouched on all fours, wearing dog leads, to perform a 'live exhibition' on a bed of gravel. But that's art. After all, no one really understood Picasso at first. At the end of the day, whatever anyone thought, people either appreciated Victor's art or it brought a smile to their faces in a world that was not always a happy place.

In Ladywood the debate raged on. There were many suggestions on how the £100,000 lottery money might have been better spent. Medical experts said it would have bought an X-ray machine with £20,000 to spare or paid the annual salary of eight junior nurses or seven junior doctors. It could have put seven extra policeman on the beat for a year or paid the annual wages of seven youth workers. It could also have funded an extra fifty nursery places. In short, it seemed that dishing out the National Lottery millions needed wise and steady hands, but instead, it appeared to be a bit of a lottery.

By April 1995 the National Lottery was already the world's largest, exceeding the most optimistic forecasts. The British public had forked out a massive £1.3 billion in the hope of becoming millionaires.

Winners had pocketed half in cash prizes – about £650 million. The government had taken a £156 million slice, while lottery organisers Camelot got £65 million and £65 million went to shopkeepers. Good causes had received £364 million, but only £31 million of that had actually been handed out.

Of every pound spent on the National Lottery, twenty-eight pence goes to good causes, divided equally between the five funds . . . charities, sport, heritage, the arts and the Millennium Fund. They get 5.6p each for every ticket bought.

Among those that had benefited in the first few months since the lottery started were The Museum of Science and Industry, Manchester (£400,000); Museum of the Chemical Industry, Widnes (£150,000); Yorkshire Dance Centre, Leeds (£606,000 to provide building renovation and improved access for the disabled); the South Bank Board, London (£980,000 to redevelop its arts centre site); Great Grimsby Borough Council (£29,500 to purchase a Steinway grand piano for the council auditorium); and the Inner Sense Percussion Orchestra, Manchester (£40,600 to buy vans and equipment for a samba band).

And so worthily on.

Sport was the first cause to benefit from lottery profits. All the grants to organisations were made for equipment, property and transport costs. In London, Middlesex University was given £186,000 to help fund a new sports complex while the Redbridge Sports Centre received £78,362 towards a new dance studio. The biggest single award went to the West Midlands, where Sutton Coldfield's Arthur Terry School, which had produced a string of athletics stars, including Derek Redmond and Phil Brown, was granted £752,600 to improve facilities. The majority of awards were under £100,000. Mobberley Cricket Club in Cheshire was the smallest, with £2,524 towards a new artificial cricket wicket. How's that!

By the middle of June 1995, lottery ticket sales, including Instants, totalled a staggering £2.3 billion. Of that sum £838 million had been set aside as prize money, creating sixty-one new millionaires since the launch. But don't panic if you feel left out. You are not alone. At this rate it would take 800,000 years for all of us to be lottery millionaires.

More than £123 million had been handed over to the five good causes, £95 million of which had been given out to 484 individual projects. Included was a grant of £23.6 million to restore a derelict castle in Dorset and £524,000 to a tennis club in Sheffield.

Meanwhile, some Cabinet Ministers weren't happy. They called for a major rethink of the way the £1.6 billion due to the Millennium Commission was to be spent over the next five years. Heritage Secretary Stephen Dorrell was spurred to take action amid growing criticism that rules for funding projects from National Lottery cash to mark the year 2,000 were in turmoil.

Labour said it would completely overhaul the system if or when it got to power, after an outcry over the way money had been allocated to the five so-called good causes.

'We want the Millennium Fund to create a vision into the next century, rather than consider every madcap scheme that comes along,' said Shadow Heritage Secretary Chris Smith. 'At present, the whole thing lacks a sense of coherence.'

Up until then, the 2,400 proposals received by the Millennium Commission had included a Ferris wheel standing 200 feet above Big Ben in London, replanting the Caledonian Forest in Scotland, cycleways, science parks, a Yorkshire pyramid and four new bridges for the River Thames.

The members of the Commission were, it seemed, disappointed at the lack of imagination behind the proposals submitted by the public. They added up to an inconceivable demand of £45 billion worth of lottery money.

Millennium Commissioner Simon Jenkins described the applications as 'slightly worthy and slightly predictable'.

He explained, 'I wanted to see more follies, more fizz, more quirkiness, more excitement. We have had Millennium towers, Millennium bridges, Millennium museums, Millennium forests and footpaths, Millennium coastlines and stadiums. There are even people asking for £1 million to think about the Millennium. We have had Millennium church bells galore, church halls are coming out of our ears and community centres comprise one-third of all the applications. The trouble is most of the applications have got round it all by calling whatever it is they want millennial.'

Many of the projects had already been rejected as ineligible because they were eligible for lottery money from the four other worthy distributors, leaving around 600 for the Commission's consideration.

Simon had the last word, 'We were asked to celebrate the Millennium and I think I share with most other members of the British nation some confusion as to what precisely that is supposed to mean,' he told the *Daily Telegraph*.

The Great Lottery Debate was well under way.

Film-maker Sir David Puttnam, a member of the Arts Council Lottery Board, joined in. He called for lottery money to provide every twelve-year-old child with a school computer. He was appalled that none of the Millennium money had been targeted at projects which could create an 'intelligent and skilled workforce' equipped to improve Britain's education, health and housing in the next century.

The criticism followed the controversial deal in April, personally approved by Prime Minister John Major, in which £13.25 million of lottery money was used to buy Sir Winston Churchill's papers.

If there was one thing the Tories could have done without in the run-up to the VE-Day celebrations, it was Winston Churchill – not *the* Winston Churchill but his grandson. His acceptance of lottery money for the war leader's personal archive had the Tories spitting blood as they faced precarious local elections across the nation. MPs said it was wrong for the wealthy descendants of Churchill to get so much. The Labour Party hit out, claiming that cash was being used to keep documents which were already national property. But Heritage Secretary Stephen Dorrell defended their purchase and said the archive had been bought for a fair price.

'There can be no better way to celebrate the fiftieth anniversary of VE-Day than to have all Sir Winston Churchill's papers secure in one place for the benefit of researchers and the public alike,' he said.

The papers ranged from tear-stained letters Sir Winston wrote as a homesick nine-year-old at boarding school to his famous 'We shall fight them on the beaches' speech of 1940. Included were no fewer than 1,040 handwritten letters from him to his mother until she died aged forty-one, and notes from every monarch from Edward VII to the Queen and from every Prime Minister from Lord Salisbury to Lord Home. The whole cost was £14.25 million, of which £13.25 million came from the National Heritage Memorial Fund, with another £1 million donated by philanthropist John Paul Getty.

There had been fears that the vast collection, which went up to the time Churchill lost power in 1945, might be sold to America or broken up. It was owned by the Chartwell Trust, which acted on behalf of the Churchill family. One of the beneficiaries was alleged to be Sir Winston's grandson, MP Winston, who it was said stood to gain several million pounds.

Other grandchildren who stood to gain from the sale were journalist Emma Soames, Countess Peel, businessman Jeremy Soames and Rupert Soames, a director of GEC. The sale of the papers had already been the subject of an increasingly bitter row. Before his death, Sir Winston instructed his heirs not to sell the documents without the consent of the Prime Minister of the day. But because he specified the Prime Minister of England, it was ruled in 1990 that this was invalid since no such post existed. The archives were housed in Churchill College, Cambridge. Papers from the years after 1945 had already been donated to the nation by Lady Spencer-Churchill. Negotiations over the future of the earlier papers had been going on since 1988, with the government making clear its desire to keep them in this country.

Churchill's nephew, Peregrine Churchill, denied the

price was excessive. 'The papers are very much under-valued,' he said. 'Their value is at least £30 million, so the nation has a bargain.'

Lord Rothschild, Chairman of the National Heritage Memorial Fund, also defended the use of lottery cash to buy the archives, which ran to 1.5 million pieces of paper housed in 1,200 boxes.

'If we had not come up with this package then I fear a large part of the archive would have been sold,' he said. 'If it had been dispersed everyone in this country would have minded dreadfully. It is surely in the same category of national importance for us as the Declaration of Independence for the people of America.'

Lord Rothschild added that the papers might have been worth even more on the open market. 'There is the possibility that the family could have got considerably more,' he said. 'I think they behaved rather generously.'

Auctioneers Sotheby's estimated the collection could have made as much as £50 million. The papers would now be made available to the public as well as academics. Exhibitions were planned for Edinburgh, London and Cardiff during 1996.

But Bernie Grant, Labour MP for Tottenham, had a different point of view. 'It's a thorough disgrace,' he said. 'Ordinary, poor people have been spending their pounds every week on the National Lottery and for them to pay £13 million for a load of words is just nonsense.'

Be fair though, Bernie. The last thought in anyone's mind as they bought a lottery ticket was the Churchill papers. The punters are only thinking about the new house and the holiday in the Seychelles.

Jeremy Corbyn, Labour MP for Islington North, chimed, 'These papers are only the product of the fact that Churchill was Prime Minister during the war and they should be part of the national archive anyway. Lottery money ought to be used to improve artistic, sporting and cultural life for ordinary people.'

Charities were left reeling by the decision which they described as 'appalling and insensitive'.

David Chesterman, Director of the British Council for the Prevention of Blindness, said, 'Winston Churchill was paid by the taxpayers to lead Britain through the war, so his items already belong to the nation. The idea that anyone would sell them is outrageous, and it's not as if the Churchill family are impoverished and would have been forced to sell them. My charity is struggling to keep things going because, as everyone knows, the National Lottery is draining money away from the charities. Conservative estimates suggest that charities will lose £200 million a year as people gamble on the lottery rather than donate to good causes. We're all up in arms about the whole thing. Any sensible-thinking person would regard this affair as a scandal. It's an absolute shock and a disgrace.'

More controversy followed when it was reported that Tory MP Winston stood to earn even more because he was retaining the copyright of the historic documents, which lasted until 2015 – fifty years after Sir Winston's death – and would make money every time one of the speeches was used commercially.

With VE-Day approaching he was set to benefit immediately. Labour arts spokesman Mark Fisher said this raised even more urgent questions about the valuation.

But Mr Churchill angrily denied allegations of profiteering by his family.

'I have no idea what, if anything, comes to me,' he said. 'All I know is that I am a potential beneficiary of this trust. People who do not have the facts at their disposal very often leap to rather mistaken conclusions.'

The MP disclosed that when his great-grandfather Sir Winston made arrangements to put his lifetime of letters and speeches in trust in 1946, he had little more to his name than the suit he was standing in, apart from the mountains of papers.

'It was his wish, when he was at a low time in his own finances, and effectively bankrupt, that they should be left to his heirs,' Mr Churchill said. 'He was seventy and at that particular juncture in his life when he did not think he had many more years to live. This was the only thing he had to leave.

'He was faced with having to sell his beloved Chartwell, which was only averted at the last minute because ten wealthy well-wishers clubbed together to buy it on the understanding that he and my grandmother would be able to occupy the house for the rest of their lives. It was his decision to put these papers in trust for the benefit of his main heirs, that is for the descendants of his only son, my late father, Randolph Churchill.'

Some of the money would go to refurbish Sir Winston's grave and other family plots at Bladon, near Blenheim, in Oxfordshire, he said. This could cost as much as £500,000.

The criticisms about the lottery cash came at a particularly sensitive time for Camelot. Charities were reported to be losing a fortune to the big draw. Voluntary donations to worthy causes had plummeted by more than £70 million in just four months since the lottery was launched and the National Council for Voluntary Organisations reckoned charities could be out of pocket by £212 million every year.

'Charities cannot compete with the National Lottery,' explained Stuart Etherington, Chief Executive of the Council.

Before the lottery began, eighty-one per cent of Britons gave money to help voluntary organisations. Now just sixty-seven per cent were.

'The relationship between individuals and charitable giving has changed,' he added. 'Fundraising methods like raffles used by large and small charities have been badly affected.'

Things were on the move. Pools firms were handed a £40 million tax windfall as the Chancellor, Kenneth Clarke, eased betting duty, while Heritage Secretary Stephen Dorrell signalled that he might come to the aid of the struggling charities. It was the first public admission by Ministers that the lottery's success had siphoned off huge amounts from other areas.

Pools companies had lost seventeen per cent of their business, jobs had been axed, and it was even predicted that one firm could fold. The Chancellor bowed to intense pressure by sanctioning a cut in the Pools betting levy from 37.5 per cent to 32.5 per cent to create a more level playing field.

The cut was hoped to boost prize funds and attract more punters. Littlewoods had axed 560 jobs during the National Lottery, while 95 went at Vernons.

As door-to-door Pools collector's days appeared to be numbered, UK Lotteries, a small charitable company, had increased takings – because of the awareness factor created by the national game. Even Leicester City Football Club had moved into the area vacated by the Pools collector and was taking its lottery on to the town's doorsteps. Other football and rugby clubs were stepping up their prize draws, which also gave the punter the chance of supporting a favoured cause.

Meanwhile the National Lottery had claimed another victim in the leisure sector – Brent Walker's betting shop chain William Hill. The company reported that the number of bets placed in its shops had plummeted 9 per cent and turnover had fallen 4.5 per cent in the first seventeen weeks of its current financial year. It blamed the launch of the Instants for the slumps, saying they competed directly with betting as both games appealed to the same punter.

At one point Brent Walker shares fell ½p to 2¾p and Ladbrokes was off 4½p to 178½p in sympathy. Ladbrokes admitted that its betting was also down. William Hill realised the seriousness of the situation after betting fell at the flagship Grand National race for the first time in living memory.

Bookmakers were keen to be involved in the sale and distribution of lottery tickets but it was a long odds shot that they would be allowed to.

Meanwhile, evidence was also growing that bingo, at one stage believed to be immune from the lottery, was also suffering. Managers reported sales down by as much as fifteen per cent.

Even Mr Dorrell it seemed, was gripped by lottery mania. The rather austere National Heritage Secretary, not recognised for his political flamboyance, was captured on camera lurking around London's Trafalgar Square, near his Whitehall offices, parading a giant cheque for good causes.

But now there was another problem. Animal and environmental charities felt they had been snubbed in the pecking order for cash handouts. Organisations dealing with children, poverty, the disabled and jobless had been included in the list for funds, along with groups concerned with women's issues and ethnic and cultural minorities. Now the animal carers and the environmentalists launched a campaign against the lottery too.

They were joined by Britain's top gambling watchdog, the Gaming Board, which had its own tub to thump. It called for thousands of teenagers to be banned from playing the National Lottery, by raising the age limit for buying tickets from sixteen to eighteen. But in spite of fears that youngsters were becoming addicted, the government ruled out a change, saying there was no evidence to support it.

Perhaps it may be worth a thought that the minimum age limit to bet at a casino or on a horse race, is eighteen.

You can please some of the people some of the time, but not all of the people all of the time. The lottery has become a subject on everyone's lips ... and there are many different views on its role in our society.

But the money keeps flooding in, and where would some in Birmingham be without it? In July two grants of almost £4 million each were among the £20 million of National Lottery cash given to the city again by the Arts Council. The prestigious City of Birmingham Symphony Orchestra received £3.7 million towards the £5 million cost of a new rehearsal hall and studios. And the controversial Ikon Art Gallery received £3.6 million towards another £5 million scheme to provide premises with improved educational and visitor facilities.

The *Sun* newspaper immediately hit out at 'barmy causes' getting National Lottery handouts claiming that the new Heritage Secretary Virginia Bottomley wanted the cash to go to medical research or to youngsters in poor areas 'rather than trendy galleries which exhibit potatoes as works of art'. The *Daily Express* called for a review of how lottery cash was handed out.

But it was the huge roll-over jackpots that were causing the most concern. Mukhtar Mohidin's £17.8 million, the £22.5 million shared by double-glazing salesmen Mark Gardiner and Paul Maddison, and Terry and Brenda Benson's £20 million win irritated some.

Labour's National Heritage spokesman Chris Smith said there was 'a strong case for arguing it would be more sensible to try to spread big jackpots among runners-up, rather than have one or two tickets winning huge amounts'.

The Methodist Church voted to urge the government to reduce the lottery's top prizes to levels below those normally offered by other forms of gambling and betting.

But Camelot, naturally, was happy with the prize levels.

'Higher jackpots mean more people will play,' the company said. 'If you reduced the size of the jackpot fewer people would play and less money would go to good causes.' They were right.

Nevertheless, Camelot was considering a second mid-week draw, which could lower the average jackpot size by increasing the number of winners.

Lottery sales were expected to hit £5 billion by the anniversary of the launch – the level originally projected for 1997.

The excitement generated by huge wins such as the Bensons' were also proving tough competition for TV rivals of the BBC's lottery show. Now ITV was planning to fight fire with fire and give away a £100,000 dream cottage every Saturday night in a new show called *Raising the Roof*.

The lottery, then, had opened a Pandora's box. What the future holds is anybody's guess. But as we all know, when it comes to money, the gods of happiness, jealousy and greed rear their heads.

The gallery of National Lottery jackpot winners, among them Mukhtar Mohidin, Lee Ryan, Mark Gardiner and Terry Benson, provided an interesting portrait of our society as we approach the Millenium. It perhaps tells us more about our way of life, our hopes, fears and dreams than many costly public surveys.